To Stuart

I hope this book blesses you!

Andy Kool

Praise for Scandalous Freedom

'One man's story……. life at the best of times can be messy. Andy's biography is a compelling read, from the highs of a professional sporting career, a lifelong addiction to porn, relationships, betrayal and the many twists and turns that his life takes.

This is a *"can't put down"* book! Andy shares and bares his heart, frustrations, pains, and consequences for his life choices – warts and all. This honest, emotional and raw story will possibly shock, surprise and evoke a different response from every reader. The ending has yet to be written and ultimately there is still hope even in the most despairing circumstances. My prayer for Andy and his girls is that God in His mercy, will trade ashes for beauty……it's not over until it's over'

Warren Evans, CEO of Sports Chaplaincy UK

'There's an uncanny familiarity for me about much of Andy's story; a life rooted in Rugby League, a West Leeds origin and a Christian faith, inspired, in part, by the testimony of the great Tommy Smales. What is unfamiliar though reveals a jaw-droppingly frank story unveiling the truths at the centre of Andy's heart, truths that he in complete faith, feels inspired to reveal. I myself became a Christian on my Rugby League journey when both Tommy Smales and Ali Lauti'iti pointed me to Jesus. My faith changed the very essence of who I was; how I tried to live and more importantly, who I was living for. The Holy Spirit drives us to live a life that glorifies Him and by His grace, we strive in the strength of His Son to discern God's will.

This doesn't make us perfect, not yet anyway. It's a daily struggle walking alongside a bar that is set at perfection, reminding us how far and deep our own sins have run. But now that we are not under the curse of the Biblical law, it's through faith we keep our face on Him, kneeling in repentance and walking towards resurrection hope, because in the end *"there is nothing hidden that will not be disclosed, and nothing concealed that will not be known or brought out into the open"* Luke 8:17

There is an openness to Andy's story which should inspire and challenge us all. It is, to me, a committed journey inspired by faith-based works. I don't think this is a book to decide judgement or argue morality, rather it's a faithful search for truth and justice'

Jamie Jones-Buchanan, Former Leeds Rhinos and Great Britain International Rugby League player

'Andy and I have common ground and a shared passion for Rugby League, Match Fishing and we are followers of Jesus Christ. To read and see the emotive journey travelled and the taboo subjects often not discussed in Christianity openly is an eye-opener and welcomed, refreshing change which is much needed within the body of Christ.

To see the power of God at work, setting Andy free in such a profound way, is just beautiful and very inspirational. The highs, the lows, nothing short of a rollercoaster journey. A journey to freedom.

Scandalous Freedom gives hope to the many of us who have felt unworthy, unloved and bound in addictions. It's a "must read" for anyone!'

Allen Langham, Speaker and Author of Taming of a Villain

'With heartfelt sincerity and boldness, Andy freely shares his incredible life in raw truth. In this challenging and inspiring autobiography, the reader is pointed towards God's love and grace for each of us on a journey, through the complexities of relationships, addiction, career and family. Thank you for your honesty'

Mike Coles, Christian Youth Leader

Scandalous Freedom ~ A True Story of Sport, Failure, Injustice and Redemption

Copyright Andy Kirk 2020

ISBN: 9798693954489

This book is a memoir and a work of creative nonfiction. It reflects the author's present recollections of experiences over time. Names, characters, identifying details, and incidents, may, in certain places, have been changed to protect the privacy of individuals. The author has recreated events and conversations from his memories of them.

All rights reserved. No part of this publication may be reproduced, stored in a retrieval system, or transmitted, by any form or by any means without the prior written permission of the author, nor be otherwise circulated in any form of binding or cover other than that in which it is published and without a similar condition being imposed on the subsequent purchaser.

Unless otherwise indicated, all Scripture quotations are from NIV, NLT, and The Message Bibles

Cover design by Loulita Gill Design www.loulitagilldesign.com

Book editing and production by The Write Companion
www.thewritecompanion.co.uk

Scandalous Freedom

A True Story of Sport, Failure, Injustice and Redemption

Andy Kirk

Dedication

To my Mum and Dad ~ I want to thank you for the fantastic start you gave me in life. For all the times you were there to love and support me. You did the best you knew how, and I will always be eternally grateful for that. I want you to know that I hold no hard feelings about anything that happened in the past. I wish you both well in your health and in your future.

To my brother, Rob ~ Thank you for being so loyal and standing by me through thick and thin. I always appreciate that! You are an inspiration to me!

To my wife Mel ~ You have been a tower of strength during the many years we have been together. Most women would have walked away a long time ago, but you have stood by me and I am proud of the marriage and family we have built. I love you with all my heart!

To Roxy and Anna ~ I want you both to know that I will always love you with everything in me. I will always be your dad and I am immensely proud of you both. I have not been the perfect father, but all I have ever wanted is what is best for you. I hope this book helps to fill in some of the gaps. We are fortunate that the movie of our lives is still rolling, so we have time on our side. I am always here for you, should either of you want to reach out and make contact.

To Zac ~ You are an amazing son and I am proud to be your dad. You will be a world-changer one day and I love being around you. You brighten up my every day.

To Harlow ~ You are my little beauty! You are so kind, funny, and super talented. I hope I can guide you through life in the best way possible. Your hugs are spine-tingling, and you make me smile and laugh every day.

To God ~ Thank you for saving me from a life of perpetual misery and destruction. I have entrusted you with my life and you have never let me down. I want to serve you always.

God bless you all.

Contents

Foreword..9

The 'Why?' Behind The Book................11

Chapter 1 ~ **Flying High!** 13
Chapter 2 ~ **Where It All Started** 19
Chapter 3 ~ **Discovering Porn** 29
Chapter 4 ~ **Learning The Game** 42
Chapter 5 ~ **Ups And Downs** 60
Chapter 6 ~ **Bombshell!** 68
Chapter 7 ~ **The Flat Cappers** 79
Chapter 8 ~ **God Sends An Angel** 85
Chapter 9 ~ **Trials and Tribulation** 95
Chapter 10 ~ **Court Battle Number 1** 105
Chapter 11 ~ **Nurturing A Blended Family** 116
Chapter 12 ~ **A Wedding And A Court Case** 131
Chapter 13 ~ **New Arrival** 139
Chapter 14 ~ **Parental Alienation** 146
Chapter 15 ~ **Back In Court** 154
Chapter 16 ~ **Enough Is Enough** 164
Chapter 17 ~ **Final Nail In The Coffin** 175
Chapter 18 ~ **Hopes For The Future** 184

Foreword

I have had the privilege of being Andy's wife for almost 8 years. His life is one of Godliness, humility, and bravery. In all honesty, in the beginning, our relationship was built on fornication and lust. Over the years God has worked through our hearts and simmered that passion into unwavering love, steadfast faith, the courage to fight the good fight, solidarity and not to forget immense laughter.

Let's not get it twisted. The marriage hasn't been without its trials. If it wasn't for the racism, the stint in jail, the lies, the police, the accusations, the pain of family betrayal and most recently, the separation of our two daughters, I do not know if we would be the power couple that stands today.

You see, Andy and I have this incredible way of dealing with adversity thrown at us. When arrows are flying at us, they just clink off our armour. That's God. Instead of allowing the poison we experienced to divide us, we decided to lean closer into each other, ultimately building the solid foundations of our marriage.

It humbles me to witness how my husband repeatedly deals with the calamities that life has thrown at him, as a rugby player, a father, and as a son. During the midst of any battle, he always remains grounded, courageous, focused, and disciplined. He is a rock, my rock! A giant - sturdy and still.

Scandalous Freedom uncovers the most profound revelations of truth any man dares to bare. It is revealing and authentic. I can honestly say that the words penned in this book are, put simply, Andy's heart exposed.

God has entrusted him with a message of hope for many men out there who may struggle with porn addiction, or the masses who may have lost connection with their children, all by the hand of deviance.

Our story is by no means over. Assuming that there are no safeguarding issues, Andy and I continue to fight for fathers to have a loving, fulfilling relationship with their children. Just like mum. In August 2020, we took ourselves down to London on an organised march. We, along with many others, stormed Parliament, to expose the hidden corruption and deception within the family courts.

I ask that once you have read this book, that you pass it on to any man who is struggling with getting access to see his children, is in despair with the family court façade, or who is tormented by the manipulative actions of previous family relationships.

You do not have this book in your possession by chance. It is by divine appointment.

Mel x

The 'Why?' Behind The Book

We live in such a sexualised world that is getting increasingly darker. As a society, we are becoming more and more desensitised to the sexualised images that bombard us daily, not just in explicit pornography, but on TV and social media. Statistics show that children are being exposed to pornography from a much younger age than previously. The average age that a child first views pornography is now 10 years old.

I am passionate about sharing with you my journey of reaching my boyhood dreams of becoming a professional rugby league player and my struggle with pornography and sex addiction. Pornography and its harmful effects are something that is still a very taboo subject in our modern society. We can all too often shy away from addressing it and that ultimately gives it more destructive power to affect our own lives and relationships.

I want to give people hope that this destructive addiction can be overcome with help from the One who made us. I want to give hope to fathers who have been separated from their children by our biased family court system and to show them that life can be fulfilling and joyful even in the midst of pain and heartache.

I hope this book will make you laugh and make you cry.

It truly is my life to date, and I believe it will help set many people free.

Andy

Chapter 1

Flying High!

It was the Autumn of 2003, which was Grand Final time in Rugby League. My career was reaching a real high very early in my career and my boyhood dreams were seemingly coming true. I was only twenty-one years old and I had made a season-long loan move from Leeds Rhinos to Salford City Reds at the start of that season, which was in February 2003. I had spent the previous five years at Leeds Rhinos, my hometown club.

At Salford that year, we had such a fantastic season. We finished top of the league in the Championship and we made it to the Grand Final via the play-off system. Only one team got promoted into Super League and it all came down to this one showpiece match at the end of the season. The winner gained promotion to Super League; the loser stayed in the Championship. So, as you can imagine, it was a highly tense and anxious place to be. What also made it so stressful, was that for all our players and staff who were full-time professionals, failure to win this one game would mean we would have to become part-time players and subsidize our rugby wages by getting another job. Nobody wanted that! Especially as most of our squad were full-time players. On a personal note, I had an amazing season that year; one of the best of my whole career. I had established myself as a regular first-team player at a new club, I scored 24 tries in 26 games that season, which was a prolific try-scoring record by anyone's standards.

However, just two weeks before the Grand Final I suffered a devastating injury blow! It was extremely doubtful whether I would make the team to play in the Grand Final. I severely injured my ankle ligaments in the dying minutes of the semi-final versus Leigh Centurions at The Willows, Salford's home ground. The Willows ground is no longer there, and the stadium has now been demolished and houses built on the land. It was one of those old traditional grounds that oozed character. It was in the middle of a rough housing estate in Salford, Greater Manchester. The changing rooms were notoriously small, and it was quite an intimidating place for visiting teams. Both the home and away dressing rooms were primitive, and the ceiling sloped with the contour of the terracing above. You could hear and feel the crowd stamping their feet above your head as you got changed to play. But the playing surface was always immaculate, and I loved playing there even as an away player before I joined Salford. My injury happened with only about two minutes left to play in the semi-final. I was running to collect a kick downfield, but as I turned to run my foot stayed planted in the opposite direction. I winched in agony and fell in a heap on the ground, motionless with not even a defender near me. I was absolutely gutted! I knew straight away it was a serious injury; I was on crutches immediately after the game as I could not weight bear on my foot at all. I knew full well that this type of injury would certainly not heal in just two weeks. My hopes of playing in the biggest game of my career were slim to none!

I don't remember much of the two weeks between that game and the final, but I remember the Head Coach, Karl Harrison, pulling me to one side at training and telling me that he wanted me to do everything I could to be fit to play in the final. Now that felt like huge pressure! I was only 21 years old and I felt a huge weight of burden on me not to let my team and my coach down. Karl was a big imposing figure of a man. He was also a 'no-nonsense', old school kind of coach who had the attitude of, "If you missed a game because of injury, then you are soft!" Karl also had a long illustrious playing career himself. He played for Hull and Halifax and represented Great Britain many times, beating the Australians in a legendary test match at Wembley in 1994. I remember watching that game on the TV as a 12-year-old lad. Jonathan Davis scored an unbelievable try in that game. Karl was the type of bloke you didn't want to get on the wrong side of either. In fact, Karl's nickname is 'Rhino', which I believe he got during his playing days for having such a thick skin that never cut. One season, after a run of bad results, we had our usual game review video session. During the meeting, Karl suddenly whipped out a massive sword. Yes, that's right! A full-on Samurai SWORD! He started waving and threatening Joel Caine, an Aussie player we had newly signed that season. He was accusing him of costing us several wins because of the mistakes he was making week after week. To be fair, Karl was right, but I'm just not sure he went about it in the right way, but that was just Karl's way! And he certainly got the player's attention on that occasion. You could see the other lads biting their lips desperately trying not to laugh just in case Karl saw them and decided to turn the sword on them. Let's just say, Joel certainly got the message! Salford brought Karl in as Head Coach from the Bradford Bulls, near the end of the previous season, to try and save the club from relegation. He did a great job, but unfortunately, the club ended up finishing bottom of the table and they got relegated from Super League. Karl knew me very well as a player. He had watched me play in the academy and first-team at Leeds while he was coaching at The Bulls. We had many close-fought battles against Bradford over the years. I believe that's why he signed me at Salford when I became available. I remember him coming to my house where I lived with my parents; he came with the club's Strength and Conditioning Coach for a chat about me possibly signing on loan. I guess it was like an unofficial interview, but he left me with the feeling that he rated me highly as a player and it was obvious that he was keen to sign me for the club. After this meeting, I felt incredibly positive about a move to Salford and my chances of getting regular first-team action, which is what I was looking for. As a club, they appeared to be extremely ambitious and determined to gain promotion back into Super League at the first attempt. I liked what I heard.

At some point, during the week building up to the Grand Final, I declared myself fit to play, even though I'd hardly trained since my injury. It was almost impossible for me to get through a full training session without physically breaking down. The club's medical team decided that I would need a pain-killing injection before the match to be able to play and possibly another injection at half time. I decided I was willing to take the risk, not just because I didn't want to let down my teammates and coach, but because I was so desperate to play in such an important match, especially after the great season we'd had. Plus, as a professional rugby player that's just what you are expected to do. *"Pain is just a sensation"* we were always taught. The Final was held at the Halton Stadium in Widnes which was quite new and modern. It held about 11,000 spectators back then and it was being televised live on the Sky Sports channel. It was the showpiece event of the season and there was a lot of interest in the game, not just from the fans, but from a wider audience outside the game too. The pressure had been on us throughout the whole season, but this was the match that counted. Failure to win this one match would mean total disaster! After the semi-final, the senior players had negotiated a nice financial bonus for each player if we got the promotion. I had played in many academy Grand Finals for Leeds Rhinos over the years, but this prize was on another level. This time the player's livelihoods were at stake! The atmosphere in the changing room before the game was a very anxious one. Everyone was just so focused on their own job and what we needed to do to win. I could hear the crowd's excitement building in the stadium; it got louder and louder as it got closer to kick-off time. As a player you try to stay as relaxed as you can, so you don't burn too much nervous energy, but it was so difficult given the prize at stake. Picture the scene from the movie Gladiator, when Maximus, played by Russell Crowe, is waiting to come up to fight in the Colosseum. It felt just like that, accompanied by the aroma of Deep Heat wafting around the changing room. I remember the club doctor coming in to give me the pain-killing injection. I think he jabbed me two or three times around my ankle, then the club physiotherapist heavily strapped it up.

I don't recall a great deal about the game; however, I know I played on the left-wing. I had played most of the season at centre, but for some reason, Karl switched me to the wing near the end of the season. Personally, my preferred position was centre. But as a player, you just play wherever is necessary for the benefit of the team. I remember my centre, Alan Hunte, scoring a seemingly impossible try out of nothing early on in the game. He chased a kick down and managed to get his hand on the ball before Leigh's winger, Leroy Rivett, could kick it out. I was so pleased for him because it was his last game before he was to retire. He had a great career, making himself a household name at St Helens in the mid to late 1990s. He was a player I really looked up to in that team. The scoreline was tight throughout the match and we got off to a good start. By half time we were 16-10 in front, but it was still anyone's game. The atmosphere was fantastic throughout the match and the stadium was packed. The fans were so loud, you couldn't even hear your teammate right next to you.

Thankfully, we went on to win the game 31-14 after we scored a late try to secure the win. I recall being happy with my own performance considering I was carrying an injury, but to be honest, it was all about getting the win and we did it! The feeling was a mix of pure exhilaration and relief when the full-time hooter went. Our dugout poured out onto the pitch, as players hugged and danced with each other and the fans were ecstatic and going crazy in the stadium. The party had truly erupted and I was determined to be at the centre of it! This would include booze, drugs, strippers, and swingers' clubs. So here I was, 21 years old, my rugby career on a massive high and I was going back into Super League with a club that really valued me.

In the weeks following our promotion into Super League, Salford offered me a two-year contract which was over double my current wages at Leeds Rhinos. It also meant I could now afford to get a mortgage if I wanted to. It was an amazing feeling! On the surface, life seemingly couldn't get any better for me.

However, there was a darker side to something that was developing fast in my private life.

Chapter 2

Where It All Began

I was brought up in the small market town of Pudsey, which is a suburb west of Leeds. I have a brother, Rob, who is one year older than me. Both my mum and dad worked hard to earn a living and to provide for us. My mum worked in a bank and she was fortunate enough to get time off work in the school holidays to look after me and my brother. She finished early during the week so she could be there when we finished school. She was a very loving mum, showing me and my brother lots of physical affection. She would always cook us traditional hearty meals which I always loved, such as Sunday roasts, Shepherd's Pie, steak with chips and peas, you get the idea, proper British food! There was a strong tradition in our house of us all sitting and eating together at the dining room table in the evening and we couldn't leave until me and Rob had eaten everything on our plate. My dad would refer to *"the starving kids in Africa"* if me or my brother tried to waste any food. This taught me a positive life lesson of not being wasteful and I have certainly taken that value into my adult life. Rob was a fussy one with food. In fact, he had a lot of funny quirks. He used to claim he had a small throat, so whenever he would eat rice, he would sit for ages complaining that the rice was getting stuck in his throat. But my dad would never let him get away without finishing everything on his plate. I really loved having an older brother growing up. We were always together as there are only 13 months between us. We would play in the garden together, out on the street on our bikes and we would practice our wrestling moves on each other on the sofa. We copied the moves from WWF wrestling as it was known back then. Our heroes were the likes of Hulk Hogan, The Ultimate Warrior, The Undertaker, Legend of Doom, the list goes on. I guess we were just doing what boys did. We had two living rooms in our house, so a lot of the time me and Rob would watch TV in one room and our parents in the other. When we would get too loud or make too much commotion, usually from wrestling each other, my dad would come in and give us a good hiding. I know times have changed now regarding society's view on physical discipline. However, I never felt that the physical discipline I received as a kid was in any way detrimental to me. In fact, looking back I feel it was good for me and my brother and it helped to keep us in line. Interestingly, me and Rob have very opposite personality traits. He is outgoing, social, and an extrovert. Whereas I am very much an introvert and I was a very shy and quiet kid. What helped me growing up was that I had a brother like Rob. I could almost blend into his shadow and let him do the talking or take centre stage. Rob had quite a severe stutter while growing up, but he never let it hold him back. My mum banned him from eating tomato ketchup because it made him so hyperactive, but it was really funny to watch! He was hyperactive anyway, without being under the influence of tomato ketchup! We must have been about seven or eight years old when we went to a Butlin's holiday camp one summer. One night at the holiday club, my brother Rob entered the 'Plate Dance' competition (not something you could get away with nowadays), which he really loved. I was watching him with my mum and dad thinking to myself, *"There's no way I would dare get on stage and do that"*. My brother always seemed super confident and fearless in a social setting. He could just be himself, something I have always admired about him. As you can imagine, as we were growing up, we were remarkably close.

My mum was such a dedicated mum and wife. She would do the lion's share of the cooking, cleaning, and household chores. I guess my mum and dad generally conformed to those traditional male and female roles within a marriage. Albeit, my mum always had a part-time job too, which developed into full-time work once me and Rob became teenagers. I think it gave her a sense of pride that she was bringing money into the household. My mum had two brothers. She had a younger brother, my Uncle Pete, and a twin brother, my Uncle Mick. Mick came to live with us for a few months when I was about eight years old. Well, I say live with us; my parents put him up in our caravan that we kept on the driveway. I enjoyed the novelty of him staying with us and we all did our best to make him feel welcome and a part of our family. He would sit and have tea with us most nights. He ended up taking me out for a run on a couple of nights a week. He liked to keep himself fit and I was well up for it! He actually taught me to run properly and he would say, *"Get your arms moving and your legs will go with them"*. He played professional rugby league himself for Hunslet in the late 1970s to the early 1980s. I am told by my family that he had quite a decent rugby career. The reason he came to live with us was that he had recently split up with his wife. She had kicked him out of the house after catching him sleeping with another woman. He was an interesting character and always came across as a very charming man. He was 34 years old when he came to live with us, and he was already on his second marriage. As I got older, I would learn that my Uncle Mick certainly had an eye for the ladies. He tended to settle down for a period, then he would usually get caught 'having it away' with another woman and that would be the end of his settled relationship. It was like he just could not help it. Later in my life, I had an epiphany moment when I realised I had inherited some of his traits, but I will write more about that later.

Growing up, I had no religious or spiritual kind of upbringing. My parents never took me to church, never taught me about Jesus or the Bible, or anything like that. The only thing I can recall was my Nana (my dad's mum), saying sweetly, *"Good night and God bless"* whenever she would put me to bed. My Nana was a Catholic. She died when I was about 13 years old. Weirdly enough though, I can always remember believing in a higher power, something that I couldn't see, but knew was good and was somehow looking after me. I can even remember lying on my bed at about eight years old, closing my eyes, and talking to God.

Dad's Skills

During my early years, up to the age of about eleven, I always looked up to my dad. I guess like most young boys, my dad was my hero. He had several jobs during my childhood. He wasn't the most academic kid at school, but he was very gifted practically, especially with his hands. I remember him having a milk round when I was young. I would sometimes go with my dad to collect the money, in his traditional milk van when I was about five years old. We went to an old lady's house and she was blind. She also had some window blinds and I remember thinking that there was some kind of connection between her being blind and having window blinds. I wondered, is that why she was blind? It is funny, some of the things you believe as a child. My dad was a bricklayer by trade, and this was his main form of employment when I was growing up. He found it extremely tough working outside in the winter months and he switched jobs to be a taxi driver for a few years. He later went on to become a building site manager but even then, he never seemed happy at work. He would regularly come home and moan and complain about one thing or another to do with work. He played Rugby League himself to a semi-professional level when he was younger and had a real passion for the game. In fact, it was he who first got me and my brother into playing Rugby from the age of six years old. He also coached our team at Pudsey RLFC until we were about eleven years old. I believe one of the reasons he encouraged me so much to play rugby was because he understood that making a living out of something you love is a real blessing. I remember watching my dad play for the local amateur team, Pudsey, when I was about five years old. He played scrum-half and was quite small for a rugby player. But by all accounts, he was a really good player and a tough one too. In one match that I went to watch him play in, a fight broke out on the pitch and my dad got kicked in the head which ended up with him being hospitalised. I went with my mum while she drove him to the hospital. He had an X-ray and the kick to the head had resulted in a fractured skull. I don't think he played much after that.

I never really appreciated how skilled my dad was until I got older. When I was a kid, he built our garage at home, which was a brick-built building with proper foundations, electricity, and a pitched tiled roof. It replaced the old garage we had, which was one of those types with pebble-dashed, concrete slab walls that scraped half the skin off your arm when you walked too close to it. It had a corrugated flat roof and me and Rob would sometimes get into trouble for climbing up on it, as it wasn't very safe. Our street mainly consisted of bungalow houses, but my dad transformed ours into a three-bedroom house with two sitting rooms and two bathrooms. That's how gifted he was as a builder. It was a pretty impressive renovation when I think back, especially as my dad did it almost single-handed.

My parents were also the first generation of their own families to own their home. This could have been due to the economic trend at the time, but it must have been a massive achievement for them. It certainly changed the course of our family generations to come. As a wise man once said, *"It's better to be an owner than a borrower"*. My dad did so many practical things for us and to me, this proved how much he loved his family. That might sound like a strange thing to say, but I don't ever recall my dad telling me that he loved me. He wasn't the type for showing physical affection such as hugging or kissing me. I think this may have been a generation attitude that was inherited or maybe my dad's father never showed him any physical affection when he was growing up either. He very rarely played with me or my brother when we were young and interestingly, when I got older, I was shocked to find out that my dad's father had died when my dad was only nine years old. I'm sure this must have been very traumatic for him at that age and possibly affected him into his adult life. When I was young, my dad had an opportunity to start up his own building business with a couple of his trusted building mates. Ultimately, they decided against it for reasons I don't know. But I really wish he had taken that leap of faith all those years ago. I know for a fact they would have been so successful and would have been inundated with building work. I also think it could have helped my dad to feel much happier at work which would have led to him being happier at home. He often seemed quite distant and unhappy. The only time he seemed genuinely joyful was when we were on holiday. It was like he turned into a different person when we went on our family holidays. He was such a fun person to be around and holidays must have felt like a real reward for the daily toil of manual labour, week in and week out.

I have so many fond memories of my childhood. I am so thankful to my parents for those memories and great times. Me and Rob would regularly play the game 'Spot' with a football on the street. It's amazing how many hours of fun you could have with just a football and a wall. We would spend hours racing on our bikes against each other and the other kids on our estate. It could get incredibly competitive too. One time, I was racing a girl who I went to school with. As we raced down our street, I edged her towards the side of the road where there was a parked car. She ran out of room and smashed straight into the parked car, knocking out her front teeth. I felt awful afterward as I'd never meant to hurt her. But our street always felt like a very safe environment to live in. There was never much trouble in the neighbourhood, and everybody got on well. However, something happened one day that still sticks with me now. I was eight years old when me and Rob were playing golf in our back garden. Our neighbour had a greenhouse in his garden which was his pride and joy! That's right, you guessed it. Golf balls and greenhouses don't mix, and I ended up smashing my golf ball straight through his greenhouse with a wayward shot. My dad was furious with me and marched me round to tell the neighbour what had happened and to apologise. Every step of that walk round to the neighbour's front door felt painful and I was in floods of tears by the time I got to the door. However, in hindsight, it was a good lesson in taking responsibility and ownership for your own mistakes, even though it felt emotionally distressing at the time.

Holidays

Holidays were always memorable times when I was growing up. We would go on at least one holiday a year, sometimes two. My parents owned a tourer caravan and I loved going on holiday to places such as Scarborough, the Brecon Beacons, Flamingo Land and Cornwall in our caravan. We had some amazing times as a family and being outdoors was something me and Rob absolutely loved. In the summer of 1991, we travelled all the way to the Isle of Wight with our caravan in tow. It was my ninth birthday while we were there, so my parents bought me a sea fishing rod and some other bits of fishing tackle to get me started. The year before, we had stayed at a caravan site on the East Coast of Yorkshire, called Hornsea. It was a pretty drab place to be honest, but the caravan site had a fishing lake on it. We went there with another family that my parents were good friends with, who were also our Godparents. They had two children, Ben and Jenny, who were of similar age to me and Rob. On one particular day, their dad took all of us kids fishing. Steve was a real kind, generous bloke and I always enjoyed it when we would spend time with them as a family. In fact, I could probably write a full book just about Ben and Jenny, and some of the bother they would get into. They were both really friendly, polite kids. Ben was a few years older than Jenny, but she used to wind Ben up something rotten. While on holiday with them in Cornwall one year, Jenny pushed Ben in the caravan site swimming pool one night while it had the pool cover over it. Then, another time, Jenny rang the fire brigade, who ended up coming out to their house, but Jenny blamed it on Ben. Then, another time, Steve asked Ben to clean the snow off his car, so Ben went into the garage, got a shovel, and started scraping the snow off his dad's shiny BMW. They would drive their parents mad, but we would be howling with laughter at some of the stories! That day's fishing in Hornsea was so memorable. I think I was the only one to catch a fish and I was mega excited! That moment sparked my interest in fishing. In fact, you could say I got hooked there and then! So, I nagged and nagged my parents for a fishing rod, and eventually, they bought me a shiny brand new one for my birthday. I was over the moon with excitement! During that summer holiday in the Isle of Wight, which was a lovely picturesque place, we would regularly ride our bikes down to the seafront and go fishing at the end of the pier. The caravan site was in a small village called Shanklin in Sandown Bay. We all had bikes, even my mum and dad, so this was a great way to explore the island as a family. For some reason, there were swarms of hornets everywhere that summer, and I ended up swallowing a few while racing along on my bike. So, there we were, all of us on the end of the pier trying to catch whatever was swimming below us. Rob was fishing with a small crab line and he ended up catching lots of small fish. He caught twice as many as I did that day! When we got back to the caravan at the end of the day, Rob was buzzing with his day's catch and he was determined to rub in the fact that he'd caught so many more fish than me with his cheap crab line. I guess you could call it sibling rivalry, but it was all good banter. Our parents allowed us to bring the fish back to the caravan so we could show off and admire our day's catch. Later in the day, my dad told us to dispose of the fish in the bin, but we were so proud of the catch that we decided to sneak the fish under the caravan, so we could admire them again the next day. We carefully laid all the fish out on some kitchen roll. But the next morning we woke up to the voice of my dad shouting, *"What's that smell?!"* Me and Rob looked at each other sheepishly, both of us knowing exactly what *"That smell!"* was! We had to come clean and it is fair to say my dad was not at all impressed with us! But it was a great holiday and I got to do loads of fishing! We also went on lots of holidays abroad too. We went to places like Majorca and Tenerife during my early years which were fantastic experiences. My parents weren't rich by any means, but they worked hard, and they really valued family holidays. It's certainly something I have adopted into my own family now as a husband and father.

During those early years, there was a strong work ethic that was instilled into both me and my brother. At the age of eleven, I would create small leaflets to advertise my car cleaning services and post them through all the houses on the street. I would charge £3-£5 per car and loved earning my own money. It gave me a great sense of pride and independence. I also managed to get a job as a paperboy when I was eleven years old, although I had to lie about my age because you had to be thirteen to officially get a paper round back then. Monday to Saturday, I would set my alarm clock for 6 am. I would run-up to the newsagents, fill my bag, and off I went on my round. I would run my whole round every morning. It took me about 40 minutes to complete before I went back home to get ready for school. It was a great way to increase my fitness too as I must have run about three or four miles every day. I received £7.50 a week to begin with which quickly rose to £10 per week. It also helped me to become streetwise as I was such a shy and quiet kid, it helped me to interact with people and become more social. I got to know many of the customers on my round and they would often chat with me or just acknowledge me with a *"Good morning"*. I think many of them were impressed with the fact that I ran my paper round every morning and even the local milkman, Harry, nicknamed me, *"Running man!"* Every year, around the start of December, I would write out Christmas cards for each of my customers. I would put their name on the envelope and write a short, "Merry Christmas" message in the card. My main goal was to hopefully get a nice little Christmas tip in the form of some cash. And it worked a treat every time. I ended up earning easily over £50 in Christmas tips alone! Happy days! However, getting up on those dark winter mornings was often tough. It certainly taught me some important key values such as reliability, being punctual, and basically the valuable life lessons, i.e. if you commit to something then you follow it through, even when you don't feel like it. It was great character building and a strong foundation to build my life on.

My eleventh year was quite a significant one. Having developed a love for fishing, my dad took me to a local fishing club that had a big junior section. The club arranged fishing matches on most Saturdays for the juniors and I began to go along in the summer months during the offseason in rugby. We would mainly fish on rivers, canals, and the odd lake or reservoir. I really enjoyed it and I slowly started to build up my tackle by either borrowing or receiving bits of second-hand tackle from people at the club. Back then, match fishing could be quite disheartening and a bit boring. We would go to some venues and I wouldn't catch anything all day. I stuck at it though, and I became fairly good at it after a while. I started to win a few matches which was really encouraging. The prizes were usually bits of fishing tackle. I won an expensive float rod in one match in York and I was buzzing! I made lots of new friends and they were great days out.

However, I was about to discover something toxic that would get a real hold on me......

Chapter 3

Discovering Porn

My childhood to date was going pretty well. I had a family that loved me dearly and I had experienced some great places whilst on family holidays. I had a nice job which enabled me to earn some decent pocket money and people in my close community started to know who I was. I had a real passion for all things sporty and I had discovered I was surprisingly good at Rugby League. Plus, I had another passion in fishing.

This was also a period in my life when I was approaching puberty. And as many kids do, I found this period of my life quite challenging. My body was starting to change, and I didn't like it! I'm sure my nose and other facial features grew at different rates and I was beginning to feel self-conscious. I thought I was starting to become ugly. And it's not just physically that I started to change, I started to feel differently too. I began to get very curious about sex. I didn't really know what sex was because I'd had no sex education at school and my parents hadn't told me anything about it either. Sex education is more available in schools nowadays but it's still an awkward subject for most parents to broach with their kids. The only information I had was from a book I'd found at home that belonged to my parents titled, 'A Good Sex Guide'. I flicked through it and I was quite amused by some of the pictures in there of women's boobs and men's bits. Then, one day I decided to rummage in the drawers under my parents' bed. It was in my dad's drawer that I discovered a collection of VHS videos. I didn't know what was on them at first. All I knew was that it must have been something I wasn't supposed

to see because they were hidden away from the rest of the videos in the house. This sparked my curiosity even more. The videos all had 'XXX' written on them. So, as soon as I got the opportunity to be on my own at home, I put one of these videos on. Wow! I was taken aback by what I saw! It was pornography! This was the first time I'd ever seen this kind of material! To begin with, it felt quite risky to be watching something that I knew I was way too young to be watching, but it was exciting too. I knew my parents would be horrified if they caught me watching it. But I felt like I was learning all about sex and how to do it. I knew most of my friends didn't have a clue about sex. My dad was obviously watching it too, so I told myself, *"It can't be that bad"*. I just watched in awe and over the following months, I watched the videos time and time again. I even started to masturbate on my own. *"Fantastic!"* I thought to myself when it first happened. I could now do what the men in the porn videos were doing, albeit not with a woman, but still, it made me feel like I was becoming a proper man! As time went on, I felt drawn to watch the videos again and again, whenever my parents were out. I also felt an urge to search for different material on the videos. I got really good at covering my tracks too. I would rewind the videotapes to the exact spot where I had started watching them, to not spark my dad's suspicion that I'd been watching his videos. And don't be mistaken, I had a few close shaves. One time, my dad came home from work earlier than I'd expected. I quickly shut down the video player and switched the channel to normal TV. I sat there, feeling very anxious. If my dad looked in the video player, he would see what was there! I was trying to act as normal as I could, hoping that he didn't look in the video player. Fortunately, he didn't, and as soon as I got the chance, I stealthily managed to move the video back into my dad's bed drawer without him suspecting anything. Phew!

I don't want to get too scientific about this, but I now understand much more about how porn addiction starts, especially for children. Most young boys and girls will come across porn at some point. However, I can now see how, as a young boy I was quickly becoming addicted to porn. When you watch porn and get aroused, certain chemicals are released in the brain. Chemicals such as serotonin, dopamine, and oxytocin. These chemicals are all part of the 'reward system' of the brain. These are also the same chemicals that are released in the brain when you take hard drugs such as cocaine or heroin. And this rush of chemicals is even more harmful to young people as the brain is still developing. As a result, the brain begins to rewire itself and create new neural pathways which are extremely damaging for children. A child's brain then becomes reliant on these chemicals, hence an uncontrollable craving for that same high which the chemicals create. That's an addiction! Whether it is porn, alcohol, drugs, or gambling, the same process occurs in both adults and children. But at that time in my life, I had no idea what was going on inside my young brain. It all felt great and I enjoyed watching the videos. In fact, I convinced myself it was a good thing and that I was simply educating myself about sex. But I was later to discover that porn is very much a counterfeit of what normal, healthy relationships are about.

Around this same period of my life, a guy who was a fishing coach at the angling club I attended, started to talk to me about sex, masturbation, and porn. It seemed a bit weird at first. This man was 25 years old when I first met him. He would often take me, and usually another lad, back to his house and show us pornographic videos. That soon developed into him encouraging us to masturbate while he was in the room and he even showed me bestiality (animal porn), which was really shocking! I never thought of it as abuse, but I can now see that this was a damaging and illegal form of sexual abuse and was designed to go further. This went on for two or three years and I even went to Ireland with him on two separate occasions on fishing holidays. Fortunately, we went with a small group of adults and teenagers from the angling club. Looking back, I can now see how he was grooming me and several other boys in the fishing club. But please understand, the term 'grooming' was not a familiar term back then and it was not fully understood like it is now. We tend to have a stereotype in our minds of what we think a paedophile will look and behave like, which is often false. These people are expert manipulators. He befriended me and he was kind and generous to me. He would often give me various bits of fishing tackle and spent time coaching me during fishing matches. I soon began to trust and respect him. But, unbeknown to me, it was all part of the grooming process. He also gained the trust of my parents too. One of the reasons I didn't say anything to my parents about what was happening, was that I feared I wouldn't be allowed to go to the fishing club and fish matches anymore. But that is just one of the fears that these types of predatory child groomers prey on. It enables them to operate undetected.

Then, I was horrified when I found via a newspaper article, that in 2014, this same man was sentenced to 11 years in prison for 23 sex offences against seven children dating back to the 1990s. When I first heard about this, I felt a strange mix of emotions. Firstly, I felt deeply saddened that so many young boys had been severely affected, and their lives had been tragically damaged by the acts of this sick paedophile. But I also felt glad that he had been brought to justice. Then this wave of guilt hit me! *"Why didn't I have the courage to speak up at the time?"*, I thought to myself. The reality is that if I had told someone at the time, I could have prevented him from harming other boys. He clearly did much worse things to other boys than he did to me. I also considered myself fortunate to have gotten away with the relatively mild abuse I had received. I had all these conflicting thoughts going through my mind. I even wondered if it was because I played rugby and I was physically big and strong for my age which prevented him from trying anything on. I will never know why, but I did feel a sense that someone up there must have been looking after me.

So, the combination of this, coupled with my discovery of porn, all contributed to the start of an unhealthy relationship with porn and sex. Over time, it twisted my thinking and my view of women. I believed watching porn was all just a normal part of growing up. In fact, as I completed my education through high school, my attitude was justified when it appeared that many of my mates watched porn too. We would regularly talk about it in quite a blasé way. During this period of my life, I was really struggling with a sense of identity and who I was. I'm sure I'm not alone in feeling this way. I know many teenagers struggle with this. My dad also seemed to be becoming more and more distant, even though he was still a constant figure in my life. He was always a great provider. Practically, he was a particularly good dad and he would continue to take me to my rugby matches and to the fishing club and encourage me to have hobbies. But emotionally, I always felt a disconnection from him. He struggled when dealing with sensitive situations, as I was experiencing during those teenage years. For example, when I started shaving at about 13 years old, I didn't feel confident enough to tell my parents about it. Anyway, one day, my dad caught me using his razor while I was shaving in the bathroom. He responded by making fun of me and mocking me in the presence of my mum. I remember feeling so embarrassed and humiliated, it really knocked my confidence. I was already struggling to trust him with my emotions, so this just created a wall and I began to bury my emotions. I was quite a sensitive kid growing up and I still am now to a certain degree. But in that moment, I'd have loved for my dad to put his arm around me and tell me that it was all going to be OK. But that just wasn't my dad's way. I understand now that he just didn't know how to be an emotionally supportive father. When I became an adult, my mum explained to me how she would often discourage him from bringing up sensitive issues I might have had, because she knew he would make a hash of it. But my dad would not take any notice of her and wade in, which would often leave me feeling humiliated. All my suppressed feelings seemed to push me further towards pornography. I think I used porn as a kind of comfort blanket, and it helped me momentarily escape from the reality of what I was feeling.

Racism

This was also a time in my life when I became aware of how my Dad would often use racist language. It was usually directed at people on the TV. He seemed to have a negative attitude towards any minority race groups, whether that be Asian or Black. He just didn't seem to like them. When the News or sports programmes were on the TV, he would sometimes shout things out, such as, "The black b******s!" I guess I got used to it after a while and didn't think much of it. It soon became very much like the norm in the environment I was brought up in. I heard my maternal grandad use similar language too and he would refer to black people as "Coons". I now know how offensive that term is to black people. I never really understood why my dad had this prejudiced attitude towards minority groups. We are all a product of our environment to a certain extent and I can only surmise that he was exposed to racist language and prejudice as he was growing up. It just shows you how racism is very much generational. Maybe the fact that he was born in 1958 and from a predominantly white, working-class area, was a factor too. From what I understand, there was certainly some racial tension in Britain during the 1960s and 1970s. I know these forms of prejudice were rife in British society. Unfortunately, his racist attitude started to rub off on me, and outside of the home, I began to adopt some of the language my dad used. It did get me into some trouble.

High School

It's fair to say that I found my teenage years quite difficult, but I don't think it was any worse for me than it was for most of my friends. I threw myself into rugby and I really started to excel at sport. We had a successful school rugby team; the coach was my Physical Education (PE) teacher, Mr Asquith. He was a tall, physical specimen of a man. He was the type of bloke who called a spade a spade, if you know what I mean? Kids at school would often refer to him as a 'meathead', but obviously not to his face. The rumour going around was that he had been in the military field before he became a teacher, but that was just a rumour and I later found out this wasn't true. He once picked up my mate Chris by the throat because he told Mr Asquith that he couldn't play in a rugby match after school. His tactics worked though, and Chris soon changed his mind and decided to play that day. We were all happy too because he was a decent player. Mr Asquith was certainly 'old school' in his teaching style! I always felt like there was mutual respect between me and Mr Asquith, probably because I was good at sport. Throughout high school, I got on well with him. He had a real passion for sport, especially Rugby League. He was also the type of man who wore his heart on his sleeve. It could get him into trouble, but I sensed he had a caring, softer side too. We won the Leeds Schools Cup Final in Year 7, my first year at high school. It was a great achievement for us and the school. The school had never won anything like that before! My parents came to watch the game along with my grandma and grandad. After the match, they took me to this old pub in Leeds city centre called 'The Prince of Wales'. It was one of those old traditional, smoke-filled pubs, full of dodgy looking characters. But I never felt intimidated in that environment, probably because my grandad knew all the pubs around Leeds well, and he seemed to know most of the dodgy characters in them too. We went to the bar and my grandad bought me half a pint of lager. I was buzzing and I felt like a real grown-up! After I'd drunk it, he bought me a full pint which I gladly supped. We didn't stay there for long but on the way home while sitting in the back of my dad's car, my head started spinning and I thought to myself, *"Wow, this is what it feels like to be drunk!"* From the age of about 12 years old, my parents never had an issue with me drinking alcohol, but they were always completely against smoking or taking drugs. I think that's how it was for them growing up, so those same values were passed down to me and my brother.

Discovering Porn

To be honest, I wasn't that keen on school. I would have been happier if I could have done PE all day, every day, although I was fortunate enough to be quite academic as well as sporty. I knew from about the age of 12 years old that I wanted to be a professional sportsman, preferably Rugby League. My parents would sometimes take me and Rob to Headingley Stadium to watch Leeds RLFC, as they were called then. They were known as The Loiners before they adopted the name Rhinos. I loved watching the likes of Ellery Hanley, Gary Scofield, and Craig Innes. They were my sporting heroes. I was also making great strides as a junior player. I was regularly getting selected to represent Leeds schools and Yorkshire schools from the age of eleven, all the way through to the Under 16s (U16s). I had a very mature attitude for my age and a real drive and determination to better myself as a player. My dad introduced me to a local gym when I was 12 years old and I started to attend a few times a week on my own. I would mainly lift weights because I knew that if I could get stronger then it would help me become a better player. The gym I started going to was called Altered Images in Pudsey and it is still there now. It was a proper bodybuilders gym so it could have felt quite intimidating for me at such a young age. There were plaques on the wall inside the gym in remembrance of guys that had died. I was pretty naïve back then, but as I got older, I realised that most of them had died from overdosing on steroids. Fortunately, I never got offered any drugs myself. Although being around adults in that sort of environment really helped build my confidence and social skills. There were some big, angry-looking bodybuilders knocking around in that gym, but they were all friendly enough to me. It gave me a real head start physically too as I was quite a skinny build growing up. I even started running my paper round with ankle weights on to help me get fitter. Anything I could do that would help in my pursuit of becoming a professional player I would do. I guess you could say I became a little obsessed, but I think it was a healthy obsession. However, I had an equally unhealthy obsession that was taking hold in my life.

Pornography continued to be a constant in the background of my life. Looking back, I can see how I was becoming increasingly reliant on the high it gave me. What is interesting about my high school years is that when the conversations with my mates would turn to girls and sex, I would always do my best to convince them that I'd had loads of sexual encounters with girls. I think most of us were lying to each other, but I felt like it gave me the kudos I craved from my peers. The truth of the matter was, I was scared to death to do anything sexual with a girl and I felt way too shy and embarrassed to try anything on with a girl.

Overall, my high school years went along pretty well, and I ended up achieving some decent GCSE grades including an A* in PE. But still, my main focus was on becoming a professional Rugby League player. I just knew that sitting behind a desk all day long would be my nightmare job! I'd also achieved the title of Yorkshire Champion in an 800 metres race when I was 15 years old. All the running I had done on my paper round from the age of 11 was paying off! But unfortunately, my winning time in the race that day was not good enough to make the English schools final. It was also looking unlikely that I would achieve my dream of signing for a professional Rugby League club. By the time I got to 15 years old, quite a few of my teammates had already signed for various professional clubs. Some had signed for Leeds Rhinos from the age of 13 years old and others were getting approached by various professional clubs. I must admit I was getting increasingly worried that I would not get picked up by a club! At the beginning of my final year as a junior player, myself and another player, Mark Calderwood, moved to Milford U16s. We had both been playing for Stanningley for the previous three seasons. But Milford had just been accepted into the National League, which was the highest level of Junior Rugby in the country. Many of the lads I played with for Leeds and Yorkshire schools played for Milford, so I knew many of them well. It turned out to be a great move and we had a successful season. We reached the National Cup Final, playing against Leigh East. I played centre that

Discovering Porn

season and Mark played on my wing. We both had great games in that Cup Final and the team managed to achieve a memorable victory. It was a great moment! I had been playing well for the representative teams for Leeds and Yorkshire schools, too. But still, all I had received was a half-hearted approach from Castleford Tigers to try and sign me on some scholarship forms. It turned out that the contract wasn't really worth the paper it was written on, so I ended up declining their offer. But I was just about to get a call out of the blue that would change my life forever…….

Crawshaw High School Team Photo (Year 7) at Headingley Stadium

Discovering Porn

Me fishing for the first time (8 years old)

A fishing holiday to Ireland with the Angling Club

Discovering Porn

Me and my brother Rob showing off our haul of Rugby trophies

My 10th birthday whilst on a caravan holiday in Newquay

Discovering Porn

Holiday on the Isle of Wight in 1991

Rugby Presentation Night at Pudsey

Chapter 4

Learning The Game

It was the early part of 1998. I was 15 years old and I was approaching the latter part of my last season as a junior player. My dad got a phone call from Dean Bell, the Head of Youth Development at Leeds Rhinos. He invited me and dad to come and have a meeting with him. Dean had just recently been appointed at The Rhinos. He was a rugby league legend and still is today. He captained the illustrious Wigan team of the late 1980s and 1990s who dominated the game in this country for many years, winning silverware year after year. He was also a Kiwi international who captained New Zealand many times. He was a tenacious player who was renowned for being hard as nails! Not long after Dean retired from playing, Leeds Rhinos signed him as their Head coach midway through the 1996 season. That was his first ever Head coach appointment, so he was very much untested. It was also the first ever summer Super League season, which heralded the beginning of a new era in rugby league. Summer rugby had arrived, which meant a much faster paced, free flowing game. This was further enhanced by the fact that all the Super League clubs were now full-time professional. But it's fair to say that Leeds struggled somewhat to adapt to the new full-time competition. They just avoided relegation in that first season by beating Paris St Germain at Headingley in the last game of the season. Dean Bell was forced to come out of retirement to play in that game and he even scored a try. I can recall standing in the famous old south stand as a 14-year-old boy, watching him score a try in the corner to secure their status in

Super League for the following season. But things didn't really pan out well during his time as Head Coach and at the end of the 1997 season, Dean was removed as Head Coach and given the role of Head of Youth Development. I was mega excited about the meeting as it could surely only mean one thing. But me being me, I tried to keep a lid on my excitement just in case it was not what I hoped it would be. I remember feeling apprehensive. I even had butterflies in my stomach as we arrived at Dean's office at Headingley Stadium. Thankfully, the meeting went as I had hoped. The club offered me a two-year professional contract. Wow! It all felt so surreal! I had dreamed of this moment from being a young boy, but if I'm completely honest I never really thought it would happen and certainly not for the club I had supported from being six years old. The deal included three financial lump sums over two years. I know some other young players managed to negotiate a little more money, especially if it was known that they had other clubs chasing them. But I didn't have that problem. I was just so thrilled at the opportunity ahead of me. My professional rugby career had just begun, and I was absolutely buzzing! Signing for Leeds Rhinos also gave me a bit of kudos. About a week later, a photograph of me signing my first professional contact with Dean Bell was in the Yorkshire Evening Post. These were the days before everything was on the internet, so a lot of local people read the daily paper. Then the same picture appeared in the Pudsey Times, so I became a bit of a local celebrity for a short while! Although I never craved the limelight, in fact, more, on the contrary, I much preferred blending in and hated any fuss, I did try to enjoy my newfound status and I know my family were all super proud. However, I was under no illusions about where I was on my journey to becoming a professional player. This was just the beginning. I had a lot of hard graft and dedication ahead of me if I wanted to succeed. But I was certainly ready for the challenge. Dean Bell was a fantastic coach and he did a great job of mentoring me. He taught me how to play the game at the next level up and he instilled a real toughness to my game. When you move from Junior Rugby to Academy level, it's a case of sink or swim. Many players struggled to make an impact at Academy level, or they just didn't have the resilience to make it through. The competition was so fierce. Back then, the Academy was Under 19s (U19s), so I was playing against lads who were three years older than me in my first season. Being an August-born baby, I was always the youngest in my year group. I felt like a boy in a man's domain. I can vividly recall my first game. We played against Wigan at the now-demolished Central Park ground. During the first half, I broke my nose while making a tackle. I stayed down on the ground while the physio came on to give me some treatment. At half time, Dean wasn't happy with me and came over to me in the changing room to give me some stern words of advice. He leaned into me and whispered, *"Kirky, when we have the ball and you get hurt, don't ever stay down. Make sure you get back in the defensive line until we get the ball, then you can go down, alright?"* With what Dean had achieved in the game and the type of tough character he was, you automatically respected what he said. That advice would stay with me throughout my career. He explained to me after the game, *"There's a difference between being hurt and being injured and when you're hurt you can carry on"*. It was a hard lesson to learn, but one I needed to learn if I was going to succeed in professional rugby league. I am so grateful to Dean for his guidance at this early stage of my development; he was a strong influence and he really helped to shape me as a player.

Previously in 1995, the club was taken over by a successful businessman named Paul Caddick, who appointed CEO Gary Hetherington to take charge of the club. It was soon uncovered that the club had some massive debts. Between the pair of them, they really shook things up at the club. They had ambitious plans which included investing heavily in youth development. Their vision was to go on and produce some quality homegrown talent for the future. It took a while, but it certainly produced fruit over the next two decades. I played with lots of players in the academy system who went on to become household names at the Rhinos. In the future, we were to find they would be known as The Golden Generation. Players such as Danny McGuire, Kevin Sinfield, Danny Ward, and Jamie Jones-Buchanan, just to name a few. As I progressed through the Academy system, I was fortunate to be a part of some highly successful teams. We won multiple Grand Finals over several years. At that time, Leeds was easily the best and most professional Academy set up in the game by a mile. After I finished my GCSEs at high school, I went on to join the apprentice scheme at the Rhinos which was expertly run by a former headteacher, Ken Bond, and Academy Coach Dean Bell. Ken was a fantastic bloke and he had a real passion to see all the young players succeed. But he had a realistic attitude and he knew that only a handful of players from each year group would manage to make a career in rugby. He sent me and a teammate of mine, Matt Diskin, to study for our A-levels at a sixth form college in Leeds. This was a three-year apprentice scheme that mixed the player's academic studies with our training and playing. It was a brilliant time in my life, and I enjoyed every moment of it. We would go to various Military/Royal Marine camps during our pre-season training. They were tough, gruelling experiences but were valuable character-building experiences. It instilled a physical toughness in me but also a mental resilience too. I would certainly need the latter in my days after rugby.

Drunken Fool

In 2001 I was made Captain of the Alliance team which was the equivalent of the Reserve team. I ended up winning the Player of the Year award that season at the club's Annual Awards Evening, held at the Royal Armouries Museum in Leeds. It was a great honour and a massive boost to my confidence. The year before, at the same Awards Evening, I totally embarrassed myself in grandstand fashion. Me and a good teammate of mine, Richie Moore, decided to start the end of season celebrations nice and early! We met at my parents' house as they were away on holiday, so it was just me and my brother with the house to ourselves. Me and Richie started drinking at about 4 pm in the afternoon. Richie was a big physical specimen of a man; he was about 6ft 3in and weighed over 17 stones. I'd played against him as a junior when he played for Keighley. He was always a big kid and he could drink a fair bit too! We swiftly downed a bottle of Peach Schnapps between us with some Aftershock shots thrown down our necks for good measure! When we arrived by taxi at the Annual Awards Night dinner at around 7 pm, we were both well on our way to being completely pissed, but me more so. To make matters worse, there was a champagne reception! That was the last thing I needed, but of course, *"It would be rude not to"*, I told myself. I quickly went from feeling relaxed and jolly to properly drunk! And my teammates knew it. But as hard as I tried, I just couldn't disguise it! I attempted to retrieve the situation by drinking a shed load of water from the bar, but it didn't seem to make much difference. By the time I sat down to start the four-course meal, my head was spinning. I was extremely intoxicated. I'd been sitting down for less than five minutes when I gingerly headed for the toilets. I staggered off with my teammates sniggering away. The moment I got into the toilet my stomach erupted and I was extremely sick! I ended up covered in vomit and it went all over the toilet and on my newly hired tuxedo. I locked myself in there for about ten minutes to gather myself. But there was no way I could go back into the main room looking like this, I was an utter mess. I was never a big drinker but after the end of every season, I would always let loose and would attempt to make up for all the weekends that I couldn't drink during the season. However, I had seriously misjudged my alcohol tolerance this time. So, I decided it was best to make a sharp exit and just hope that no one would notice I had gone. I don't know why, maybe it was the 'Tight Yorkshire Man' in me, but I decided to catch a bus. I ended up sitting on a bus with my head hanging down between my legs with no idea of where I was heading! I looked up to find that I'd been sick down the whole length of the bus. How I managed to not get kicked off the bus I will never know. But thankfully I somehow made it home. I woke up the next morning feeling like I had been hit over the head with a hammer. My pride was also slightly dented due to the fact I had made a drunken fool of myself in front of my teammates and club officials. I just hoped no one had taken much notice of the state I was in and that it would just get swept under the carpet. Well, I was massively mistaken. When I turned on my phone, I had a few voice messages from Ken Bond. When I eventually plucked up the courage to ring him back, he wasn't best pleased! But to be honest, he was more concerned about my welfare than anything else. I'm not sure if he saw me that night, but he had heard about the drunken state I was in! He genuinely thought I had fallen into the local River Aire and been swept away. The next time I saw Ken it was a bit awkward, to say the least. I felt bad that I had just disappeared that night, causing him so much worry and concern. But I took my lecture on the chin and we moved on. Looking back, I think the wisest decision I made that night was to bail out and head home. The lads certainly enjoyed giving me some stick about that night for a long time after!

But despite this embarrassing incident, I was beginning to make my mark within the club. I was building a reputation as a player with the potential to progress further. I'd found my best position was at centre, but I could also fill in on the wing and even at loose forward. I had been selected to represent Yorkshire Academy on a few occasions and I was selected for the Great Britain Academy Squad. I made some great friendships during those first three years at Leeds Rhinos. I hit it off well with Jamie Jones-Buchanan. Jonesy, as we called him, was a local lad and like me, he had played at Stanningley before signing at the Rhinos. He was in the age group above me, but interestingly we both shared the same passion for fishing. While we were in the Academy, we would go off in the summer and do a bit of fishing together. Jonesy is a real character! He is one of the most intelligent, deep thinkers I know, but he wasn't blessed with much common sense when we were younger. On our way back from a fishing session in York, Jonesy was sitting in the passenger seat of my Fiat Bravo. I had a six-disc CD changer in the boot of my car, so I had a few CDs in the glove compartment. Jonesy picked up a CD and proceeded to try and slot it into where the cassette tapes went. He looked puzzled as to why the CD wouldn't fit and I wondered what on earth he was trying to do! That was just some of the daft stuff he would do. Jonesy was always super competitive too, but he could sometimes get a bit overzealous. During the 2002 pre-season, we had just signed a giant prop forward from St Helens in the figure of 6ft 9in tall Wayne McDonald. During a training session, Wayne decided to test himself against Jonesy. They were both grappling each other in a tackle when out of the blue, Jonesy threw a right hook, which landed bang on Wayne's chin. It made an almighty crack and I could hear the blow from the other side of the pitch, where I was standing. Wayne didn't make himself particularly popular when he first joined the club, so the rest of the lads found it hilarious! Little did we know at the time, but me and Jonesy would go on a similar spiritual path in the future, but I will get to that later.

In contrast, Kevin Sinfield (Sinny), did everything to perfection which gained him the nickname of Peter Perfect among the lads. Sinny had been touted as a top prospect from a young age and he was mature beyond his years. He was good mates with Barrie McDermott as they car shared to training from Oldham. Barrie would often rib Sinny for not coming out for a beer with the lads after a game. Sinny would insist on going home to rest and ice his bumps and bruises. That was how professional Sinny was throughout his whole career and it was that professionalism that helped him become a club legend.

My First Lads Holiday

At the end of my first full Academy season, one of my teammates, Mark Calderwood, arranged a two-week holiday to Tenerife for the lads. It was 1999 and I was just seventeen years old. This was going to be my first holiday away without my parents. I was really looking forward to it, especially after the perpetual grind of training and playing all season. I joined ten of my teammates on a plane to Tenerife. As you can imagine we were all proper giddy! We were on our first holiday away without our parents, but we managed to get to our destination without too much trouble. We stayed in the party destination of Playa las Americas which had a reputation for being wild. And we certainly were not disappointed. Our accommodation turned out to be considerably basic but that didn't bother us. I mean what could we expect for just £250 each for our flights and accommodation? If you can, picture the scene in The Inbetweeners film, where they turn up at their grotty, run-down hotel. In fact, the whole holiday was a bit like that film. However, the hotel had a massive swimming pool which was a bonus! You couldn't make this up, but our hotel was situated directly next door to a brothel! So, after a heavy night out on the booze, some of us would fall into the next door 'establishment' before crashing out at our hotel. They would advertise that a live sex show was on in the early hours. I went in on a couple of occasions with some of the other lads and it was a real eye-opener into what seemed like a very seedy underworld. But to be honest, my years of viewing porn had very much desensitised me. Plus, as a teenager, during family holidays to Benidorm with my parents, I had seen a bar and night club performer called Sticky Vicky. She was famous for pulling all sorts of strange objects out of her vagina. Playa Las Americas certainly lived up to its reputation as a place for sun, sea, and sex. Anyway, after a week into our holiday, we arrived back at our hotel from a day out to find that all our rooms had been ransacked! We were gutted! Strangely though, our room doors were still locked, so it was clearly an inside job. Most of us had jewellery or money taken from our rooms. It put a real downer on the holiday and six of the lads decided to book an early flight home. Fortunately, I didn't get any money stolen because I'd had the sense to rent out a safe deposit box. But there was no way I was going to let those thieving scumbags spoil my one and only holiday a year. I was definitely staying, and I made that clear to the other lads. To be honest, I think for some of the lads it was a convenient excuse to go home as they were missing their home comforts! So, eleven became five and we made the most of our second week in Tenerife. After a boozy two weeks, we were all utterly exhausted! I formed some close bonds with some of the lads on that holiday that will stay with me forever.

Super League Debut

At the start of the 2001 season, I was 18 years old. I had played in several first-team friendly matches. They were usually held in pre-season on Boxing Day and New Year's Day. The league season didn't start until February so most players including myself, hated playing in these matches. They served no real purpose in gaining match fitness, as the start of the season was still months away. It was an untimely interruption to pre-season training. However, it was nice for the fans and supporters to get out and watch a game and it was a way for the club to generate some money during the offseason. However, as a young, inexperienced player, it was an amazing opportunity to test myself against established, first-team players, and I relished the opportunity. In fact, during the festive friendly matches of Christmas 2000, we played against Castleford Tigers and Halifax. We had made a few big-money signings that season including Australian internationals Tonie Carroll, Bradley Clyde, and Brett Mullins. The latter two players were at the back end of their careers and I was in awe of them. They were players I had watched as a kid growing up, playing in test matches on the TV. I wasn't the most confident player at this stage of my career, but something happened in these matches that really boosted my confidence. First of all, I played well, and I scored a pretty decent try against Halifax. Tonie Carroll was on the bench in that game and he was due to come on and replace one of the centres as that was his specialist position. But the coach at the time, an Australian called Dean Lance, put Tonie on in the second row. The day after the game, I read the Rugby League paper's report on the game. It was always interesting to see what the sportswriters had made of the game. Dean Lance made some interesting comments about why he brought Tonie Carroll on in the second row rather than in the centre. His comments read, *"Our two young centres, Andy Kirk and Chev Walker were playing so well that I couldn't take either of them off"*. Dean's comments were a massive boost to my confidence.

I was also welcomed into the first-team squad by the likes of senior players, Francis Cummins, Barrie McDermott, and Darren Fleary. They were all top blokes and I think they knew how daunting it was for a young player like myself coming into that environment. Franny and Barrie were great at getting the squad together to socialise and they would organise some great social outings. There was still a distinct drinking culture in the game at this time. Mad Monday, as it was known, was usually a boozy all-day affair, that took place the day after the last match of the season. There was one Mad Monday session that stands out in my memory. We did the famous Otley Run in Leeds, in full fancy dress. The Otley run is basically a pub crawl about three miles long from Headingley to Leeds City Centre. I dressed up as Spiderman and I had a Lycra mask covering my whole face, so it looked brilliant, but wasn't so great for drinking in. It stunk to high heaven by the end of the night. Drinking games were a big part of the day, with Franny being one of the senior players leading them. It was a hilarious day! In one pub, Keith Senior and Tonie Carroll had to do a naked run around the pub, as a forfeit. Needless to say, we all got kicked out. Then Anthony Farrell and Marcus St Hilaire ended up in a scuffle with a group of students. However, a few days later, the club received a visit from the police. The students had recognised who we were and reported the incident to the police. However, Gary Hetherington managed to smooth everything over by getting the players involved to apologise to the students.

I eventually made my Super League debut as an 18-year-old in a match at Headingley versus Hull in April of 2001. Both the club's international centres, Keith Senior and Tonie Carroll were out with injuries, so Dean Lance gave me the nod. He expressed to me that he had 100% faith in me and that I was more than capable of doing a good job for the team, despite my youth and lack of experience. However, before the game, I was a nervous wreck! I got this overwhelming anxious feeling that I wasn't good enough and didn't deserve to be there. I was burning up and I couldn't calm myself down. It was like a panic attack that I couldn't control. I had never felt anything like it before. I was trying my best to disguise the anxiety from my teammates. The game was being held on a dark, cold, and wet Friday night and the pitch was waterlogged. In fact, both me and now Leeds Rhinos legend, Rob Burrow, made our Super League debuts that night. We were both 18 years old. I started in the centres and Rob came off the bench as a substitute. We ended up narrowly losing the match, but I got through the game OK without making any glaring mistakes and my defence was sound which I was glad about. However, I struggled to make much of an impact offensively in the game. I think my nerves held me back somewhat, although Rob scored a fantastic try that was to become his trademark. If you don't know Rob, he is only 5ft 5in tall and many experts within the game disregarded his chances of making it as a Super League player, mainly due to his small stature. But Rob used his size to his advantage throughout his career. He was so quick off the mark and he would duck under tackles to break the line and beat defenders. And he did just that on his debut by scoring a brilliant individual try out of nothing. He did the same thing in his second match the following week when playing against Warrington Wolves which was broadcast live on the Sky Sports channel. I started that match in the centres again and although I had a solid game, I again failed to make the same impact that Rob did. Funnily enough, it was during that game that Sky Sports commentator, Mike 'Stevo' Stephenson, nick-named Rob 'Beep Beep' after the cartoon character 'Road Runner', because he was so quick. At this time of writing, Rob has just been diagnosed with Motor Neurone Disease (MND). At this moment in time, there is no cure for MND. My heart goes out to Rob and his family. Unfortunately, after the match against Hull FC, Dean Lance was given the sack. I thought it was a bit harsh considering the club had several experienced senior players out of the team because of injuries. But being involved at clubs where coaches got sacked, was something I would soon get accustomed to. The club appointed recently retired Rhinos player, Daryl Powell, as the new Head Coach. By the end of the 2002 season, I had made around 15-20 Super League appearances in the first team, but I was getting increasingly fed up with my lack of first-team opportunities. I couldn't really complain. I was only 20 years old and I was playing at probably the best Rugby League club in the country. Plus, on top of that, playing in my position at that time were some fantastic international players who were established superstars of the game. Another exceptional young talented player, Chev Walker, who was a similar age to me was also at the club and he was impressing with his performances. But as a professional sportsperson you always want to push yourself and play at the highest level you can.

Loan Move

At the beginning of the 2003 season at Leeds, me and my dad arranged to meet the Rhinos CEO Gary Hetherington, to request a possible loan move to another club. I loved being a Leeds player and playing for my hometown club was all I'd ever dreamed of doing. But I felt I was ready to play regular first-team rugby and that wasn't happening for me at the Rhinos. I had always found Gary pleasant to deal with and the meeting was positive. Gary had a reputation of being, let's say, a bit stingy when it came to negotiating player's wages. But I do believe that is one of the reasons why the club went on to become so successful on the pitch, as well as financially stable after Gary took over as Chief Executive. He introduced a strict policy and pay structure whereby he would never pay a player more than the club could afford or what he thought they were worth. I signed my first full-time professional contract at Leeds when I was 18 years old after I had been an apprentice player for three years. I was only getting paid 12k a year salary, plus bonuses for first-team appearances and any international selections. Hardly rolling in money, eh? But that was generally what the young players at Leeds got paid for their first full-time contract. Gary also took advantage of the fact that for most young players, it was their dream to play for Leeds Rhinos, plus many of them were still living at home with their parents so he knew they didn't need a lot of cash. During that meeting, Gary was very understanding of my ambition to play regular first-team rugby. He kindly offered to contact other clubs to see if there was any interest in taking me on a loan spell, as I was still contracted to Leeds for another year. Fortunately, two clubs came in for me, Halifax and Salford. Halifax were in the Super League at the time, but they were really struggling financially and had recently lost a lot of particularly good, experienced players. Many experts in the media were predicting that Halifax would be the whipping boys for the upcoming 2003 season. So, I ended up choosing a season-long loan move to Salford, who had just been relegated the previous season. Fortunately, they had managed to keep a full-time playing squad which was going to make them strong contenders to bounce straight back up into Super League. It panned out perfectly and I gained a wealth of experience at Salford. I quickly established myself in the team and we gained promotion back into Super League. The season was probably the most memorable of my career. We won the Northern Rail cup as it was known then, which was the League Cup and I managed to score a crucial try in that game. We recorded a club record score against Gateshead, beating them by 100-12. The record still stands to this day. But to be honest, emphatic wins like that are not the kind of games you remember. I even became a bit of a fan's favourite that season and they made up a song. I first heard them singing it during an away game about two months after I joined the club. I had scored an 80-metre solo try in one game and as I was walking back to the restart, I heard this chant coming from the stands, *"Andy, Andy, Andy Kirrrrk, Andy, Andy Kirrrrk......."* I mean, it must have taken them ages to come up with that song! Nevertheless, it was nice that they'd acknowledged my talent in this way.

During my loan season at Salford, I was reacquainted with a guy called Tommy Smales. I first met Tommy when I was 18 years old when he was assisting the physiotherapy team at the Rhinos. I suffered from a few different injuries that first season at Salford, but thanks to Tommy's healing hands, he helped to keep me fit and on the field. Tommy was no longer working at the Rhinos, but he was still working as a physiotherapist. It was my coach at the time, Karl Harrison, who advised me to go and see Tommy for treatment. Tommy was the landlord of a pub in Featherstone, West Yorkshire. He was the landlord there for many years and it was only about 30 minutes' drive from where I lived. He used his living room upstairs in the pub as a treatment room. Karl knew Tommy well. Karl had been on the receiving end of Tommy's healing hands during his own playing career. To be honest, Tommy was an absolute legend in rugby league circles, not only because of his expert knowledge as a physiotherapist but additionally, he was a great guy and a really interesting character. Tommy would soon become like a father figure to me and a massive influence in my life.

Promiscuity

The day after we won the 2003 Grand Final to gain promotion, an almighty party was arranged by the players. These types of end of season blowouts were quite common and could go on for days. However, the relief the whole club felt after gaining promotion made this party even bigger! Firstly, as was a custom at all rugby clubs, any player who had failed to score a try that season would have the forfeit of doing a naked run around the pitch. Now, this was tame, as, at some clubs, the senior players would make players do their naked run around a bar or pub, which usually ended up with them getting kicked out. A few of the senior players also arranged for some strippers to come and perform at the club along with a karaoke machine. Apparently, the stripper thing was a club tradition. This is probably a good time to mention more about how I was handling my obsession with pornography. The truth is, I was now watching porn as frequently as every day and it had become an unhealthy daily habit. The reality was that I was now addicted to porn, although I still couldn't recognise it. I was also being influenced by being in the predominantly male environment of a rugby team from the age of fifteen. It had contributed to my perverse mindset towards porn, sex, and women. Some of my experiences up to now had managed to convince me that watching porn was normal and that most guys indulged in it. Whilst playing at the Rhinos, a player brought in a porn DVD one day and all the lads sat around and watched it. We all thought it was great and a right laugh! And that was just how normal porn was perceived in that environment. So, having some strippers come to our end of season party at Salford didn't feel weird or sleazy in any way. In fact, a visit to a strip club was a regular occurrence on a night out. More and more, I was viewing women as sexual objects.

I noticed a few things during that first season at Salford that opened my eyes to some of the unprofessionalism that went on at some clubs. I guess you could say I had been spoilt by the highly professional operation at Leeds Rhinos, on and off the pitch. At Salford, the medical treatment seemed very substandard compared to The Rhinos. Players were regularly provided with painkillers in order to get through training sessions and games. There were also little or no rehabilitation programmes for injured players. And that was just the start of it. Our end of season boozy celebrations eventually led into Manchester city centre where I was shocked to witness that at least two-thirds of the squad were in and out of the toilets for most of the night taking cocaine. Now, maybe I was a little naïve, but I'd never witnessed this kind of drug-taking during player's nights out at Leeds Rhinos.

A handful of the players also regularly visited a swinger's club in Manchester. They would often tell stories about their exploits at the swinger's club and what kind of things went on. Most of the lads would find their stories quite amusing. However, it all sounded like a very seedy world that they were involved in, but I could hardly judge! They invited me and another player along that night. We'd never been before, so we were very apprehensive, to say the least. We gave fake names to get in and we were given a little white towel to wear. I was seriously considering bailing out at this point, but *"in for a penny, in for a pound"*, I thought to myself. Thankfully, the place was dead, as it was a Monday night. However, it was a massive eye-opener into what appeared to be a very sleazy world. The main room had a bar area with sofas positioned around a big screen TV, which was showing porn. A few rooms were coming off from the main room. There was a games room, some rooms with beds in and a room with a jacuzzi and a shower in. Me and my mate decided to chill in the jacuzzi, while our teammates chatted in the bar area to some regulars. After 20 minutes or so of relaxing in the jacuzzi, me and my teammate decided we'd seen enough and left the other lads to it. We got a taxi back into Manchester and joined back up with the rest of our teammates and proceeded to get on the pull.

The years of viewing porn from such a young age were having a distinct influence on me. From my late teens to early twenties I became extremely promiscuous. I began sleeping around at any opportunity I got, usually while holding down a regular girlfriend. You could say, I wanted to have my cake and eat it. I knew full well that my behaviour was morally wrong, and I felt guilty about it. But I would somehow manage to convince myself that it meant nothing and as long as my girlfriend at the time didn't find out, then in my mind, I wasn't hurting anyone. A pattern began to emerge in my intimate relationships from the age of about 17 years old. I'd get into a physical relationship and I would generally feel happy and settled for a while. Then I would start to sleep around. Without a doubt, my main objective on a night out with my teammates or friends was to get laid! It felt like an uncontrollable, compulsive desire. The drinking culture within rugby league was rife at that time and I gladly embraced it, although, I could always control the level at which I drank alcohol and it never became a problem for me. However, I definitely used it to boost my confidence in a social setting. As I have already mentioned, I have always been quite shy and a natural introvert. I would feel very awkward and uncomfortable within social environments. Alcohol helped to lower my inhibitions and it gave me the confidence to talk to women on a night out. It also helped me to come across as outgoing and chatty. I learned from observing some of my teammates too and how they would approach and speak to women during a night out. At Salford, all the players were given passes to an exclusive club in Manchester, called The Press Club. It was a strange place. To get inside you had to walk down some stairs into the underground club. As you entered, there was a long bar that only served cans, bottles, and spirits. The music came from a duke box. Not a flash, pretentious place at all, and it would stay open all night. But it was like a who's who of celebrities. They could go there, chill out, and not get bothered by fans. We would go there once everywhere else had shut and I remember seeing Rio Ferdinand in there and the actor who played Roy Cropper in Coronation Street. I must admit, I was a bit starstruck, as I was a big fan of 'Corrie' back then!

Although my promiscuous, womanising ways felt great at the time, the buzz was always short-lived and time and time again it would leave me feeling empty and unfulfilled. But then once the feelings of guilt and shame of being unfaithful had subsided, I would repeat the same pattern. As I indulged in this sexually immoral lifestyle, I subsequently opened the door to other immoral behaviours such as lying, deception, and manipulation. It's fair to say that any sexually immoral person is also, more than likely, to be a liar. To be able to maintain this lifestyle, I had to sneak around and be deceitful. But let's face it, I had mastered the art of being deceitful since the age of 11 years old when I first started watching my dad's porn collection. There's no doubt I had developed an appetite for 'sneaking around sex'. But I would soon discover that this desire would never be satisfied.......

Tenerife 1999 - Made some great lasting bonds on this holiday

Chapter 5

Ups And Downs

My rugby career seemed to be progressing well and I had settled into my role nicely at Salford. During the weeks following the club's promotion to Super League, they offered me a two-year contract. I was delighted at the opportunity and signed the permanent move. Leeds Rhinos demanded a transfer fee for me even though I was out of contract at Leeds. Unlike in football, where the well-known Bosman ruling allows players to be free agents when they are out of contract, in Rugby League the rules are different. If a club had developed a young player and that player is under 24 years old and was being offered the same money as their previous contract, then the club was within their rights to demand a transfer fee. Gary Hetherington was a smart bloke when it came to business, so offered me the same deal I was already on, which enabled Leeds to demand a transfer fee from Salford. So, in the end, Salford paid £15,000 to Leeds Rhinos for my registration. I guess that was only fair, given that Leeds Rhinos had developed me as a player from the age of fifteen. The main goal in our first season back in Super League was to avoid relegation. We managed to do that and ended up finishing ninth that season, which was mission accomplished. I played most of the season on the wing, which wasn't my preferred position, but I felt I did a decent job in a struggling team. I managed to score five tries in 20 games that season, not exactly prolific for a winger but reasonable for the matches we won. We beat Widnes at home in the first game of the season, then we went on a ten-match losing streak. This put us under massive pressure! Our coach, Karl Harrison, was highly regarded as one of the best English coaches in the game. He was even touted in the media as the next England coach. And although I thought Karl was an incredibly good defensive coach, I found that he tried to coach some of my natural ability out of me. For example, I had a unique way of carrying the ball in one hand between my hand and wrist. It enabled me to flick the ball to my winger when I drew in defenders. A bit like the classy Aussie centres, Matt Gidley and Jamie Lyon. But Karl didn't like it as it wasn't the textbook way to hold the ball. I felt my personal development as a player suffered under Karl. I also managed to continue with my womanising ways and during a ten-night pre-season training camp to Jacksonville, Florida, I made the most of the downtime we were given at night. But it wasn't long before the bubble was about to burst for me in a cruel way at Salford.

Rejection

Before the 2005 season had even started, I received some devastating news from the club. The Football Manager at the club, an Australian called Steve Simms, pulled me into his office one day after training. Now, just to let you know, there is a salary cap in Rugby League and at this time the rule was that each club could only pay 20 players a salary of £20k or more per year. When I had signed my two-year contract the previous year, I was in this bracket of 20 players. During the meeting with Steve Simms, he informed me that due to some of the new signings the club had made, they now had 21 players earning more than 20k per year. He told me that if the club registered all those 21 players for the upcoming season, then the club would be breaching the rules of the salary cap which would result in the club being heavily fined or deducted points. This was either a major f**k up by the club, or Steve knew exactly what he was doing! I firmly suspected the latter, especially given Steve's reputation as a bit of a snake in the grass if you know what I mean. He went on to tell me that between him and the coaching staff, they had decided to choose me as the player they would not register, based on the new signings they had made. I was in total shock and disbelief at the situation. It took me a while to get my head around what was going on. The reality was I could not play at all for the club during the upcoming season even though I was contracted for another year. It was utter madness, and I couldn't believe what I was hearing! Steve told me I was well within my rights to still turn up for training and get paid for the remainder of my contract, but that I would not be able to play a single game that season. The injustice of the whole situation rocked me to my core! Especially after all the hard work, I had put in to get into this position in my career. The time period after I received this news was mentally tough and so emotionally draining. I believed that Steve Simms had premeditated this behind my back. I couldn't help feeling aggrieved. My motivation to turn up and put in the hard graft at training quickly faded away. It was a disgusting way to treat anyone, especially a young player. But to find the positives, it taught me a hard lesson early on in my career about just how callous clubs could be. It made me realise that I was just a piece of meat to the club and there was no sentiment involved in these types of decisions. My maternal grandparents had always been so supportive of my rugby career. They came to every single one of my games without fail and they were always on hand to offer me advice if needed. I am so grateful to them for that and they offered encouragement and support during this difficult time in my career! I expected that my dad would find it difficult. Whenever these types of setbacks came along in my career, he would get terribly angry and bitter, to the point where it would be emotionally exhausting to be around him. He struggled to understand how I could stay positive when I was being treated so unfairly. But I'd learned from a young age to find the positives in the most testing of times. On this occasion, we were in the living room at home talking about the situation when he said something to me that stopped me in my tracks. He said with a tone of admiration, *"Andrew, you're an extraordinary person, nothing ever seems to bother you, and you seem to take everything in your stride……".* It was the first time I'd ever heard my dad speak so complimentary of me in this way and it took me by surprise. He was wrong in one respect because it certainly did bother me, but he was right in his observation of my ability to take things in my stride. Everything inside me wanted to say back to him, *"It's because I believe in God and I believe that everything happens for a reason"*. But I just didn't have the courage to say it.

Over the years, fear had built up in me that he would laugh or humiliate me if I expressed my own personal beliefs, especially anything spiritual which he always seemed to disregard. I was also scared that he would tell everyone that I'd lost the plot. You see, my dad had no faith in God whatsoever. I think it had something to do with him being made to go to the Catholic church by his family as a young boy. I believe he wasn't treated very well by the people involved, from what my mum told me.

Fortunately, I had an agent who was also a sports lawyer. His name was Richard Cramer and he was renowned in the game for being the 'go-to' man when it came to disputes between a player and a club. He took on many cases where players were in contractual disputes with the club and he was passionate about the well-being of the player. I liked Richard, as he always seemed to be on the side of the player and would fight your corner. He was the sort of guy you wanted to be on your side in this situation. After many weeks of to-ing and fro-ing between Richard and the club, he advised me to hand in my resignation to the club. We decided to take the club to an employment tribunal for constructive dismissal. This is basically a situation where an employee has no other option than to resign because of the way they are being treated by their employer. The timing of this whole situation couldn't have been any worse. It was now mid-January, with the season starting at the end of February, which meant that most of the Super League clubs had their squads full. Many had no room left on their salary cap to sign any players. However, Richard was very well connected within the game and he managed to get me a deal at Wakefield Trinity Wildcats. It seemed quite a good move at the time. However, I had to sign a significantly reduced contract on a one-year deal with the hope that I could mitigate my financial loss in the tribunal against Salford. And even though Wakefield had finished in the top six in Super League the previous season, it personally felt like I was taking a step back due to the rejection I felt, although I was grateful for the opportunity given to me by the Wakefield coach, Shane McNally. He knew me well and rated me highly as a player. And at least I no longer had the tedious journey from Leeds to Manchester on the M62 motorway to training every day. I could now really get my teeth into some hard training and attempt to settle into a new team and get to know my new teammates.

But my time as a Wakefield player would be short-lived. On a personal note, the season started off well. I established myself in the team and I was either starting games or coming off the bench. I had the privilege of playing with some world-class players at Wakefield that year, players such as a Samoan named David Solomona. What he could do on a rugby pitch was unbelievable! He was a second-rower, but he had the skills of a half back in a forward's body. About halfway through the season, I suffered a knee ligament injury in a reserve team game against Wigan. It took me about eight weeks to fully rehabilitate the injury, by which time the coach, Shane McNally, had been sacked. The expectations were high from finishing sixth the season before, but the club found itself battling at the wrong end of the Super League table. The assistant coach at the time was Tony 'Casper' Smith, who took over as caretaker coach. Tony didn't have a lot of experience in coaching and had only recently retired from a successful playing career. Tony pulled me into his office not long after he took charge. It was like déjà vu! I sensed what was coming. Tony clearly didn't share the same opinion of my playing ability as Shane did. He explained to me that other players were in front of me in the pecking order and that I was unlikely to play again that season. It was another tough rejection to take, but I respected Tony's decision and his honesty. He could have easily kept me hanging around until my contract expired at the end of that season. He even offered to have a word with the club

Chairperson to try and make the club pay the remainder of my contract, so I could become a free agent and find another club straight away.

Halifax RLFC

By this time, my tribunal case against Salford for constructive dismissal had been and gone. To my dismay, I was unsuccessful. Steve Simms and the club's barrister played a blinder. At the hearing, they managed to convince the panel that they had tried their utmost to find me another club. It was just another kick in the teeth, but at least I could put it all behind me now. I'd managed to negotiate a payoff deal with Wakefield, and I signed for Halifax RLFC who were in the Championship, which was the division below Super League. My agent, Richard Cramer, negotiated a good short-term deal for me until the end of the season. Only three games were remaining before the play-offs. Halifax had ambitions of gaining promotion to Super League after a two-year exile from the top flight. The coach at Halifax was also an old teammate of mine from Leeds Rhinos, Anthony Farrell, or 'Faz' as he was known. He knew my game well and he knew he would get nothing less than 100% from me! If I were describing myself as a player, I would say I was a tough, hardworking centre. I prided myself on my defence in the game and I did a lot of unselfish work in both attack and defence. At times, I was probably too much of a team player and didn't do enough to stand out as an individual. Faz was probably one of the best coaches I had throughout my whole rugby career. He wasn't the best tactically, but he was a great manager. I played some of the best rugby of my career while under his tutorage. He knew exactly how to make me tick. He never tried to tell me how to play, he simply told me to play my natural game and spoke positive words over me. I remember when I initially signed for the club, that the local paper, The Halifax Courier, reported on me joining the team. I remember reading the positive words that Faz had spoken about me to the reporter. It filled me with confidence, and it gave me the motivation to go out and perform to the best of my ability for him. The playoffs came around and the team we're playing with boatloads of confidence. We were riding on the crest of a wave. We reached the semi-finals of the play-offs and we were up against Castleford Tigers who were the favourites to gain promotion that season. Castleford had also tried to sign me when I left Wakefield just a few months before. The game was a really tough encounter and I injured my top rib when I got dumped to the ground in a big tackle. But I managed to play on through the pain. We were two points in front with just ten minutes to play and just moments away from a Grand Final place. But they scored a try in the opposite corner with only five minutes left to play and we narrowly lost the game. We were devastated because we'd come so close! Castleford went on to comfortably beat Whitehaven in the Grand Final a week later and gained promotion to Super League. I loved my brief time at Halifax, and I jumped at the offer to stay at the club and signed a one-year contract for the following 2006 season. I played with one of the most skilful players I've ever played with during my time at Halifax. He was an Australian half-back named Ben Black. He was a maverick type player, but also a loose cannon off the pitch too. We gelled well on the pitch and complemented each other's game. Halifax was a part-time club, but the deal I signed was enough money for me not to have to find a part-time job. However, I ended up embarking on some schools coaching for the club, and for a couple of days a week, I worked as a labourer on the building site that my dad managed. The new season came around quickly and I continued my good form from the previous season. But despite my own personal good form, we were struggling around mid-table, which was not where we were expected to be. The club had serious ambitions of promotion that season. With about ten games to go that season, Faz was given the sack. I was gutted for him! This was becoming a familiar story for me and I was beginning to wonder if I was the curse? Halifax brought in a new coach straight away. It was ex Wigan hooker, Martin Hall. I didn't know anything about Martin, but it soon became obvious that he wanted to shake things up at the club and put his own stamp on the team. About three-quarters of the playing staff weren't offered new contracts. And despite me winning the Halifax Evening Courier Starman Award at the End of the Season Awards night, I was also informed that my services would no longer be required by the club. Once again, I was massively disappointed and the familiar process of finding another club would begin. But I was about to receive some news in my personal life that would literally turn my life upside down……

Chapter 6

Bombshell!

While I was playing at Wakefield Trinity Wildcats in 2005, I decided to enrol on a course to learn to be a driving instructor. I felt I needed to have another income source prepared for when I did finally retire from Rugby League. I was fully aware that Rugby League was going to be a relatively short career and I understood that if I did drop down into the Championship, I would have to supplement my income with another job. A driving instructor seemed like a great job that could work alongside my rugby career if needed. I would be able to work my own chosen hours as much or as little as I wanted. By the time 2006 came around, I wasn't yet a fully qualified driving instructor, but I had passed my first two exams which meant I could work as an instructor with a trainee license. I was twenty-three years old and one of my students was a lady in her forties. On the surface, she appeared to be a genuine lady and she used her charm and seduction to win me over. I was later to discover that not all was as it seemed with this woman, but I will explain more later. Anyway, she soon introduced me to her daughter, Josie.

Josie was a year younger than me and her mum did a good job playing matchmaker. To be fair, I didn't take much persuading, even though I was already in a relationship. I arranged to go out with Josie for a drink. I continued to see her over a few weeks and one thing led to another. Inevitably, our relationship became physical. This was all happening while I was already in a long-term relationship. The familiar pattern of my relationships quickly unravelled. I ended up calling it quits with my long-term girlfriend and started a new relationship with Josie. It's shameful to think how these intimate relationships with women had become so easily dispensable. As soon as my feelings changed, I was selfish enough to simply dispose of that relationship and move on to the next woman.

Josie and I had only been together for about three months when I received a text message that would change the course of my life forever. I still lived at home with my parents at this time and I was sitting at the dining room table eating one of my mum's favourite home-cooked meals, steak, chips, and peas. Midway through the meal, my phone beeped with a text message. I opened the message to discover a text message from Josie. She was telling me that she was pregnant! My heart momentarily stopped, and I felt like I'd been hit by a train! I instantly lost my appetite, and everything seemed to be going in slow motion. After ten minutes or so I managed to gather my thoughts and start to think about how I was going to respond to this unexpected news. I tried to remain positive about how we were going to deal with this bombshell news that had landed in our world. In the days that followed, we sat down and talked about how we were going to handle this situation. It was tough because, to be honest, I felt the relationship would have run its course after a few more months. But I desperately wanted to do the right thing for my unborn child's sake. Fortunately, in the 12 months following me signing for Salford, I had bought two modest terraced houses that I rented out. I'd always been astute with my finances, so I bought the houses as investments for the future. So, we decided we would move into one of the houses. I issued the tenant their eviction notice on the property I owned in Bramley, Leeds. This meant we could at least try and make a go at being a family. The house wasn't flashy by any means; it was a small three-bedroom terrace house built in the 1920s with a small back patio. So, we moved into the house in September of 2006. Josie was given a due date of 29 January 2007. I began to really embrace the thought of being a dad, even though it was completely unexpected. I had always envisioned having a family of my own one day, so why not now, I thought.

However, moving out of my parent's house gave me new freedom and my porn addiction certainly rose to a new level. I now had my own space and my own home computer with high-speed internet. I was watching porn as frequently as every single day, sometimes for hours at a time. But I still didn't even consider that I could be addicted. The thought never crossed my mind, plus, I hadn't known that you could be addicted to porn. And like most addicts, I was very much in denial. I ignored the fact that I might have a problem that enabled my behaviour to continue. Despite me now having a baby on the way, my porn addiction had slowly developed into sex addiction and my habitual sleeping around with various women was getting out of control. I don't mean this to sound patronising, but this is probably a good time to define what addiction actually is.

"Addiction is not having control over doing, taking or using something to the point where it could be harmful to you. An addiction gets out of control because you need more and more to satisfy a craving and achieve the "high". Addicts will continue with the behaviour despite the negative consequences"

(Taken from the internet)

This is a concise explanation of what addiction is, without going into the science behind it.

Josie's due date, the 29 January 2007, came and went. So, the doctor booked her in at the hospital to be induced on Monday 12 February. Back then, the doctors wouldn't allow pregnant women to continue the pregnancy for more than 14 days over their due date. But on the night before, Josie's waters broke, so we rushed down to St James hospital in Leeds, late that night. After a long labour, our daughter was born on 12 February 2007, at just after five o'clock in the afternoon. Wow, it was an amazing feeling! I know it sounds clichéd, but I'd never felt a love like it in all my life! As I first held her tightly in my arms, the overwhelming feeling of love and a sense to protect her was so powerful. As I tried to dress her in the hospital for the first time, I was so worried that I might hurt her, she was so small and delicate. I really embraced fatherhood and I absolutely loved having a precious baby daughter. It did take a bit of getting used to though, but Roxy was such a good baby. During that first week at home with her, there were moments when I even forgot she was there. I was making some dinner while she was sleeping in her Moses basket in the living room. Then I heard this quiet whimper coming from the living room. At first, I thought it was on the TV until it dawned on me that it was Roxy crying! Being a dad was even better than I thought it would be. I don't really like the saying, 'hands-on dad' as I feel it can be quite patronising to any loving father who just gets on with things and does what they're supposed to do. But I was *very* hands-on, and I would get up in the night to do the feeds, I would change nappies, I would take her to the nursery and pick her up, take her to dance class, all the stuff that makes being a dad so enjoyable! I used to hate leaving her at nursery too as she would cry and cling on to me.

Another Year ~ Another Club

By now, my rugby career had moved to Widnes Vikings and I once again found myself travelling over the Pennines from Leeds for about five days a week for training. Fortunately, Widnes were a full-time club, even though they were in the championship. For that 2007 season they had splashed out on some quality players and promotion to Super League was a genuine goal. It was at Widnes that I made friends with a real sporting hero of mine, who I looked up to immensely, a kiwi player called Toa Koa Love. Toa was a really tough player, but he was also a very classy centre, who had spent most of his playing career in England at Warrington Wolves. I'd played against him a few times in Super League. He was nearing the end of his career when he signed for Widnes, but he still had a lot to offer. He was a good guy too and I made a firm connection with him during that season, even though we were rivals for the same position. Toa ended up getting a five-match ban during that season after he knocked out an opposition player with one punch during an altercation. However, it turned out to be a great opportunity for me, as I got an extended run playing in the right centre, which was always my best position. There was a small group of us who travelled over to Widnes daily. We were nicknamed "the Yorkshire bus" which included, me, Scott Grix, Oliver Wilkes, and Andy Cain. Travelling as a group was a great way to keep the travel costs down but it also helped to ease the boredom of the long journey, which was a 140-mile round trip. I have some very fond memories of the Yorkshire bus and we all brought our quirky character traits into the journey which never failed to make it entertaining. Grixy loved his music so he was the Bus DJ most of the time. However, my time at Widnes opened my eyes to some of the performance-enhancing drug-taking that existed in the game. I realised I'd been quite naïve to some of the things that went on. There were two players that I knew of in our squad that were taking Human Growth Hormone (HGH). One of the players was quite open with me about it. And if what I was hearing was true, it was rife in the sport. The main purpose of taking HGH is to help the body to recover more quickly, allowing players to train harder and for longer. It's a natural hormone released in the body, but taking it helps to boost those levels in the body, which then becomes unnatural. It was during this season that the UK Anti-Doping Agency (UKAD), introduced random blood testing for Super League players. This would help them to detect higher than normal levels of HGH in a player's system. But for Championship players, they still only had standard urine tests that did not detect HGH. Taking performance-enhancing drugs was never something I had thought about doing and I certainly didn't agree with other players doing it. However, looking back, I do believe I would have had a better rugby career if I had. The coach at Widnes was a guy named Steve McCormack, who was a top bloke and he was well-liked by the players. Steve was an experienced coach and he was also in charge of the Scotland rugby league team. Steve was another great 'people person' who had this innate ability to get the best out of his players by giving them the confidence and freedom to express themselves on the field. I loved my time at Widnes, and we had a successful season. We made it to the Grand Final against Castleford Tigers which was played at Headingley Stadium, a familiar ground for me. We had beaten Castleford in each league match that season, so we were the bookies' favourites going into that game. However, I was gutted not to be selected to play in the final, but I managed to take it on the chin as it wasn't unexpected. Steve had done a great job of keeping a quality squad of players happy that season by rotating the squad regularly. But I was always going to be the second choice for the centre position as we had Toa in one centre and the other centre was a huge Cumbrian lad named Mick Nanyn. Mick was built like a prop forward but once he got motoring, he could move a fair bit too. He scored tries for fun and was the team goal kicker too. Sadly, we got beaten in the final which meant we'd failed in our attempt to gain promotion. It was a tough loss to take, but that's the harsh reality of sport at the highest level. However, we were soon to discover that the defeat was to have much wider consequences for the club. The day after the Grand Final, we all went out on the typical end of season boozy session in fancy dress. We did our best to drown our sorrows and cheer ourselves up. A few hours in, we heard a rumour that the club had gone into administration. It turned out to be true which effectively meant the club did not have to pay us and we were all free agents. The news was a colossal blow for all the players and staff at the club. It left us in a position of uncertainty regarding our futures. In the weeks ensuing the club's announcement, some players decided to take a risk and wait for a new investor to buy the club, but other players decided to look for another club. I really wasn't sure what to do, but I knew I needed to get away on holiday and enjoy some downtime with Roxy.

Home Life

Roxy was only nine months old when me and her mum took her abroad for her first holiday. We went to the Canary Islands and I loved being with Roxy! It was a real haven for me to spend time in the sun, playing with her on the beach and in the swimming pool. It helped take my mind off the stress of rugby matters. On the surface, my relationship with Josie seemed like a normal, functioning relationship. We had now lived together for just over a year and we had a beautiful nine-month-old daughter. However, the truth was, we barely knew each other when Josie became pregnant. We were only now really beginning to get fully acquainted with each other. It was beginning to dawn on me that we had truly little in common. I've always had lots of different hobbies and interests, but she didn't seem to have any interests or hobbies. She would think nothing of ridiculing my interest in fishing. She had this habit of gathering some of her friends and family around at the house and have what I can best describe as a good old gossip about anyone and everyone. I found it difficult to be around this type of atmosphere and it created negative energy in the house. I told her how I felt, but it made no difference. I think it was normal to her and what she'd been used to being around. I certainly didn't want to rock the boat too much, especially as I loved being a dad to Roxy! This was also a period when I started to discover that Josie's mum had some disturbing character traits too. We would often go over to Josie's mum and dad's house for Sunday dinner and other family social events. This is when I noticed how her mum would speak to her husband in a disrespectful, contemptuous manner. It was to the point that it made me feel extremely uncomfortable. I would go so far as to say it was a form of emotional abuse. There was clearly no love between them, and I started to wonder just what Josie's dad had done to deserve this level of disrespect in his own home? Josie, her brother, and sister also seemed to join in with their mum's behaviour. At times I felt so sorry for her dad as he was a quiet, passive bloke. He would just sit there and take it. It frustrated me at times because I really wanted him to stand up to her! Then, I noticed a pattern, when every so often, after months of sitting there and taking the abuse from his wife, he would get drunk and lash out at his wife. Now I never actually witnessed him do this, as it would usually be late at night after he'd been out and had a skin full. Josie's mum would then cleverly play the victim, by phoning the police and reporting him for domestic abuse which would sometimes end up with him spending the night in a police cell. Now, I am not condoning his actions, but my perception was that he was the one who was the victim of mental and emotional abuse from his wife. Josie, along with her brother and sister, would also take their mum's side which I always found strange! But Josie's mum was the more dominant figure in the house, so everyone else seemed to align with her. The 'game' that Josie's mum was playing was quite sickening to witness and I had never experienced this type of family dynamic before. It certainly sent alarm bells ringing in my mind!

But I was hardly able to judge on morality with my secret flaws. I was practically living a double life at times with my porn and sex addiction. It was reaching a peak in my life and there were days when I would watch porn for hours at a time. I could easily masturbate between 10-15 times in the space of an hour. It would get to a point where I would be in physical pain, but l would still continue to masturbate. The sex addiction was an extension of the porn addiction. I had reached a "jumping off" point, where I felt I needed to do the acts I'd seen in porn to achieve a greater high. Being able to flick from one scene to another while watching internet porn, simply fuelled my appetite for sex with lots of different partners. The thrill and the buzz of the variety were too powerful to resist. I was craving the next high, and just like in porn, I could click to a different scene or genre at the touch of a button. But that insatiable desire in me would never be satisfied! I had made women and sex an idol, but even more concerning was the fact that I was totally blind to the power it had over me. However, all this was about to change with a miraculous encounter…

Halifax Courier Starman 2006

Playing for Leeds Rhinos 2002

Salford Reds Vs Wigan Warriors in Super League 2004. I sustained a broken nose!

Bombshell!

Playing at Salford in 2004

Leeds Rhinos 2003 team photo

Chapter 7
The Flat Cappers

When I returned from our holiday in the Canary Islands, my agent told me that Featherstone Rovers were interested in signing me, so he arranged a meeting with the board of directors at the club. To be honest, I was getting sick and tired of moving clubs now and I desperately wanted to settle at a club. The other problem with continually moving clubs is that you have to prove yourself afresh to the fans, so it always used to feel like I was starting from scratch again. It can also give you a reputation as being a problem player who maybe had a bad attitude or who caused fractures within a team. But that certainly didn't reflect me. Featherstone had just been promoted into the Championship after a dominant season. Rovers fans are known as "the flat cappers" due to the town's reputation for being a typical, working-class, Yorkshire coal-mining town. It also comes from the area's renowned love of pigeon racing and keeping ferrets. If you have ever seen the 1970s comedy film, 'Kes', well, that sums up the people of Featherstone. Honest, hardworking people who call a spade a spade! It was one of the most bizarre ways I'd ever negotiated with a club. Me and Richard arrived at the club on a dark mid-week evening. We went into the board room at the famous Post Office Road ground at Featherstone. There were about six or seven board members in the room including the club chairman, Mark Campbell. Mark had been a supporter of the club from his childhood. But he was also a local businessman and a real character! During the meeting, I quickly noticed that Mark had an ear missing, which I couldn't stop staring at! I kept thinking, *"How on earth did that happen?"* Mark and the other directors expressed to me their plans for the club going forward. He was committed to ensuring that the club would be successful, and he had an ambitious plan to take the club into Super League, which had never happened before. He was also willing to invest a large amount of his own money into the club. It all sounded incredibly positive. Oddly, they put a contract in front of me that they wanted me to sign there and then! Richard negotiated some of the terms, which the board agreed to. But I didn't feel comfortable signing a contract without having some time to sleep on it. So when I expressed to the director's my wish to take some time to think about the offer, Mark piped up, *"Andy, if you sign the contract now, I will come over to your house tomorrow and bring you some cash, how's that for ya?"* I believe that's called, 'sweetening the deal'! Mark knew that I was out of pocket from what had happened at Widnes. The fact that Widnes had gone into administration meant I had lost two months' wages. So, I agreed to sign the two-year contract there and then. I was now officially a Featherstone player. And true to his word, Mark came over to my house the next day with a wad of cash for me. But what was even more bizarre, was that he came in his shiny red Ferrari. We spent about 30 minutes chatting in my living room, but I couldn't help thinking that someone might try to break into his car. I mean, you don't see many Ferraris in Bramley! But I did find out how Mark had lost his ear. Someone had decided to bite it off in a fight while he was on a night out with the players the previous season. I was starting to wonder what sort of club I had got myself into!

I was now a part-time player, so I needed to look for another job to supplement my rugby wages. I was on quite a decent wage for a part-time player, but I decided to get a part-time job at Royal Mail as a postman. I had visions of it being like when I was a kid doing my paper round. It seemed to tie in well with my rugby as we trained two or three nights a week at Featherstone and usually played on a Sunday. I also loved being closer to home, as it meant I could spend more time with Roxy which I absolutely lived for! I could pick her up and drop her off at the nursery too.

That first season at Featherstone in 2008 went well. I was the first choice to play centre at the club and I started the season playing reasonably well. However, it was the first time that I had ever experienced such a toxic atmosphere within the dressing room. There were two, maybe three players, who loved to have a moan and a grumble about anything and everything. It created a dark energy that I found draining and it was difficult to be around. The 'coach curse' seemingly struck again and with about nine games still to go that season, our coach, David Hobbs, was given the sack. I think it was a harsh decision but I had become so used to coaches getting sacked that it literally seemed a normal thing to encounter. The team was around mid-table, but I think Mark Campbell and the board of directors expected more, considering the money they'd spent bringing players to the club. The club brought in an experienced Super League coach in the shape of ex Huddersfield and England coach, Jon Sharp. The players didn't really take very well to Jon and I could see why. He came in with a very arrogant attitude. I got the impression that he believed he was too good to be at a club like Featherstone and that he was doing us a favour by being there. But he was technically a very astute coach and he did get more out of the team. During one of his first games in charge, I completely tore my bicep tendon off my bone while making a tackle. It happened just 20 minutes into the match, but I carried on playing. The physio could see I was struggling, so she came on to give me treatment and I told her I was in a lot of pain. I knew it was serious. About two minutes later, the physio came back on and told me that Jon had said to her, *"Tell him unless he has broken his arm, he can't come off!"* That might sound harsh, but as a rugby player, you are always taught to play through the pain barrier. It was what you were expected to do. Plus, we had no backs on the bench in that game. I played the rest of the game with my bicep tendon torn and completely detached from the bone in my lower arm. I was literally a passenger for the rest of the match, but I managed to get through the game, and thankfully we won. But that was the least of my worries! The club physiotherapist misdiagnosed the injury as being more minor than it actually was. So, I ended up playing the rest of that season with this horrific injury. A lot of injuries that rugby players get are remarkably similar to car crash victims because of the impactive nature of the sport. I was heavily strapping my arm up and popping strong pain killers just to get through each game until the end of the season. We ended up finishing the league season in eighth position, which was outside the playoff places. But I was just so relieved that the season was over! I took some time off before the next pre-season began. One positive aspect of me now playing at Featherstone was that my good friend and mentor, Tommy Smales, literally lived around the corner. I'd been receiving treatment from Tommy ever since I left Leeds almost six years earlier. He had now moved from living in his pub to a house just over the road. He set up his treatment room in a spare room and rugby players from many different clubs would regularly visit Tommy for treatment. But this bicep injury was even beyond Tommy's healing hands.

Fortunately, a new physiotherapist was appointed by the club. He suspected that my arm was much more seriously injured than the previous physio diagnosed. He immediately sent me to a specialist surgeon at a private clinic in Manchester. It was a guy named Dr Funk, who had an excellent reputation in the sporting world for fixing these types of injuries. I walked into his office and within about 30 seconds of assessing my injury, he confirmed I needed an operation immediately. However, he explained to me that because the injury had been left for so long, without it being accurately diagnosed, it would be a bigger operation. He also said that it may never heal back to full strength. I was astonished when he explained to me, *"We have two options. I can take some tendon from your thigh and graft it into your arm, or I can order a bicep tendon from a dead person? But that's risky as your body might reject it"*. Wow! What a decision to have to make at 26 years old!

He suggested the first option and I was happy to go along with that. He booked me in for the operation a few weeks later, on 12 December 2008. They put me under general anaesthetic and Dr Funk and his team did what they needed to do. I woke up from the operation and was immediately violently sick. I think it was the side effects of the anaesthetic. The recovery period was expected to be about 6 months before I would be fit enough to play again. That was a huge blow, but there was nothing I could do about it. I had to just focus on my rehabilitation now. I was also forced to take some time off from my job at Royal Mail but fortunately, I was entitled to sick pay. After the 2008 season at Featherstone, they appointed a new head coach. It ended up being my old coach from Leeds, Daryl Powell. Daryl was an excellent technical coach with a wealth of experience coaching in the Super League. It was a great capture for the club. However, for me personally, I could see the writing was on the wall. I knew Daryl didn't rate me very highly as a player and I knew that was why he had allowed me to leave Leeds Rhinos five years earlier. Then, just two days after my operation I received a phone call from my agent. Richard explained that Mark Campbell had been in contact with him and he expressed a wish to terminate my contract with immediate effect. Wow! Talk about kicking a man when he's down, eh? I'd put my body on the line for this man's rugby club. I'd pushed myself through the pain barrier and risked my life and limb (literally!) Now, they were telling me that they wanted to wash their hands of me. I had long ago come to realise that there was little loyalty from a club towards a player, but this felt like a brutal decision. I was furious and I immediately arranged a meeting with Daryl Powell. I suspected he might have also been behind the decision. I told him in no uncertain terms that the club was bang out of order and that I was well within my rights to sue the club for negligence. The way they'd misdiagnosed my bicep injury was terrible. Daryl took on board my frustration and he understood my position. I let Richard know that if the club were willing to pay me the full amount of my contract then I would agree to terminate my contract. But I knew they didn't want to do that. They wanted to pay me a miserly amount to simply get me out of the way. Fortunately, between me and the club, we managed to patch things up and we agreed that I would stay for the remainder of my contract. I'd always had a strong mental attitude throughout my rugby career, so I decided to focus my energy on knuckling down and working hard to get back to full fitness as quickly as possible. It paid off and I managed to get extremely fit and back into the team by April, which was two months ahead of schedule. To be honest, it was a little too early in my rehabilitation process. But I was just itching to get back playing and among the lads.

Chapter 8

God Sends An Angel

I've mentioned Tommy Smales a few times already, so let me elaborate on my relationship with him. Tommy played rugby in the 1950s and 1960s for Featherstone, Huddersfield, and Bradford Northern. He played scrum-half and he was quite a diminutive, but a highly intelligent player. He had an illustrious career as a player and captained both Huddersfield and Bradford to Challenge Cup victories. He also represented Great Britain on several occasions. Tommy made an immense impression on me from the minute I met him when I was 18 years old at Leeds Rhinos. He was a real character, a very kind and generous man who just loved people. I got the sense that he was vastly different from anyone I'd ever met before. He wasn't at the Rhinos for long before he left as he was there helping out with the physiotherapy and sports massage side of things. After I left the Rhinos, I was reacquainted with Tommy while I was playing at Salford in 2003. Tommy was 68 years old then, but he was super fit for his age! I started visiting him at his pub in Featherstone where he had been the landlord for over 20 years. Initially, it was for treatment on a hamstring injury that I couldn't shake off at that time. He managed to heal my injury in no time and I soon realised why he had such a renowned reputation in Rugby League as the go-to man to get you fit from injuries. After that injury had healed, I began to book in with Tommy for a sports massage the day before every game, without fail. I would drive over to the Travellers Rest pub which was about 30 minutes' drive down the M62 from where I lived in Leeds. Tommy was unbelievably knowledgeable and skilled at what he did, considering he was predominantly self-taught. Whenever I would ask him where he learned his healing skills, he would often reply with, *"God showed me"*, which used to annoy the hell out of me, as I wanted a straight answer. He would often spend as long as 90 minutes treating an injury, using mainly hands-on treatment and a few machines, which to be honest, looked like they belonged on The Antiques Roadshow! But what he did always worked! Tommy had this unusual technique of using his ultrasound machine on an injury, while the injured body part was submerged underwater in his bathtub. His theory was that the ultrasound worked more intensely in water. I'm not too sure how effective it was, but Tommy's track record at healing injuries was so good that I trusted him 100%! And I knew so many other top rugby league players trusted him too. I would regularly bump into various Great Britain Internationals at Tommy's, such as Lee Gilmour, Barrie McDermott, and Paul Sculthorpe. He even helped Ellery Hanley through some injuries in his playing career. His sports massages were brilliant too and it made a substantial difference to how my body felt going into the game. My legs would feel lighter and he loosened my muscles so much so that I noticed I was faster and stronger during a match. After years of receiving sports massage from Tommy, I just couldn't have imagined playing a game without having a massage from Tommy the day before. I simply wouldn't have felt ready to play. He even started to teach me about sports therapy. He would sometimes ask me to work on his back or his legs after he'd finished treating me. He told me what to do and I was only too glad I could help him. Tommy didn't have much concept of time either, maybe it was his age, but I would regularly turn up for my appointment and he would still be treating someone else, but I didn't mind waiting as there would always be some colourful characters in the bar area to keep me entertained. Tommy had some hilarious sayings too. For example, when he wanted you to turn over on the massage couch, he would always say, *"Roll over, Beethoven!"* He would use ice and soap to massage me with. His theory was that by using ice, he could work deeper into the muscles. Before he would apply the ice on my skin he would say, *"Twice as nice with ice!"*

And whenever he would lose track of the time he would say, *"Time flyeth, Goliath!"*

Tommy just loved people, especially rugby people, and he would regularly tell stories from his playing and coaching days. In fact, Tommy would tell me the same stories time and time again. I knew them off by heart. Even if I'd say, *"Oh yes, Tommy, you've told me about that before"*, it didn't stop him. He just loved recalling those memories and telling those stories. And I loved listening to them. I knew the joy it brought to him to tell those tales. He suffered slightly with his short-term memory, but he could remember the details from past events like it was yesterday. It was obvious how much he treasured his time playing and coaching rugby. He loved his family dearly and he would often talk about his son, Russell, and his daughter, Lisa. I also know that his grandson passed on when he was very young which he would often talk about.

Spiritual Side

Tommy had a distinct, spiritual side to him too and it was evident from the moment I first visited him at his pub, how much his faith meant to him. And he certainly wasn't afraid to share his faith with other people. The first time I walked into his living room for a treatment, he had the Bible open on his massage table. He would read it in between treatments. He would also have his TV broadcasting from the GOD TV channel too. He shared with me about his profound supernatural experience of when he was 'born again'. I think many people would have run a mile, but I was fascinated with his life-changing experience. He used to say to me, *"You're very open-minded Andy, I can't talk like this with everyone"*.

I'd always believed in God from as young an age as I could remember, but I never really had any context or reference to help me understand how God fitted in with Jesus and the Bible. I remember the Religious Education (RE) lessons at school were always extremely dull and it was mainly an excuse for a mess about in class.

But when Tommy would tell me about his faith it seemed so genuine and tangible. He explained to me how his faith wasn't so much to do with religion, but how everyone could have a personal relationship with God through his son Jesus if they wanted to. My ears would prick up when he spoke about his faith and I would listen intently and ask questions. He would quote Bible verses that I can still remember now, like,

> *'As a man thinks in his heart, so is he'* Proverbs 23:7
> *'There is life and death in the power of the tongue'* Proverbs 18:21
> and,
> *'Sweet words are like a honeycomb, sweet to the soul and health to the bones'* Proverbs 16:24.

Tommy had this amazing ability to relate the Bible to everyday life, in particular to my rugby. And it all seemed to make sense to me. I began to realise that this ancient book was still so truly relevant today in our modern society. It blew my mind and I began to ponder on the idea that maybe it was all true! Did the God who I believed in and spoke to in my bedroom as a kid, actually exist? One of Tommy's favourite Bible subjects was the end times and he was absolutely fascinated with what the Bible had to say about the end of the world and about how Jesus was coming back one day. I loved listening to him talk about it all. I'd never heard anything like it before, but again, it made sense to me. By now, I'd been visiting Tommy for regular treatments for almost seven years and we'd created a real friendship. To be honest, he was more like a father figure to me and I respected him immensely. I genuinely believe that God powerfully used Tommy to influence the course of my life.

Meanwhile, back at home, I plucked up the courage to express some of my newly found Bible knowledge to Josie. But she flippantly replied with, *"Oh no! You're not gonna turn into one of those Bible bashers, are you?!"* But I should have expected no less from her. It's fair to say that she had zero interest in any kind of spiritual matters. One day she came home and saw me watching a programme on GOD TV. She pulled a disapproving face and said, *"What's this s**t you're watching?!"* I felt so humiliated and it put me off sharing my newfound spiritual beliefs with her.

Tommy had shared with me about his own supernatural experience of when he became born again. He shared how he received the Holy Spirit and felt like he was being filled with a liquid love from his head to his toes. He even heard the audible voice of God. It all sounded so spiritual and quite miraculous! I'd never heard of anybody experiencing this before, but I believed his story. Tommy explained what the Bible said about the way to live an eternal life with God in heaven and that all I had to do was believe in God's Son, Jesus, that He died on the cross for my sins, and to invite Him into my heart. He told me about a conversation that Jesus had with a religious leader named Nicodemus about how to receive eternal life with Him in heaven. Jesus explained to him, *"I tell you the truth, unless you are born again, you cannot see the Kingdom of God."* John 3:3. Although I fully believed in Tommy's experience and believed that there is a God, I was still somewhat apprehensive about the Jesus thing. I was scared that if I invited Jesus into my heart and I didn't get the same experience that Tommy had, would that mean God had rejected me? And I was even more concerned about what people would think, especially my own family. I'd imagined them getting the men in white coats to cart me off to be sectioned! And then there were my teammates. I didn't know anyone who ever mentioned about having a faith in God. It just seemed so alien to anyone in my circle. But I also felt so lost in my personal life; I knew morally I was a mess! I was living a double life at times in order to cover up my porn addiction and womanising ways. And how would that change if I were to become born again? All these questions and insecurities were running wild in my mind.

Born Again

Anyway, one day at home during the middle part of 2009 I decided to give the Jesus thing a go. *"What have I got to lose?"*, I thought to myself. I went into my bedroom when Josie and Roxy were out, and I knelt down with my elbows on the bed and closed my eyes. Why I did it like that I don't know, it just felt like the right way. My words went something like this, *"Dear God, I believe in Your Son Jesus and I invite you into my heart. Please forgive me for anything I have done wrong in my life and please show me that You are who You say You are, In Jesus Name, Amen"*.

It was simple as that and I truly meant it. I opened my eyes, looked up, and paused. I didn't feel any different, no goosebumps, nothing. I was half expecting to see a blinding light or maybe some angels dancing on my duvet. *"Come on God, give me some sort of sign"*, I thought to myself. So off I went, thinking that I'd wasted my time on this Jesus thing. And I certainly wasn't going to tell anyone what I'd just done. I'd have felt like a right tool!

Stirring

At this stage of my life, my porn and sex addiction were rampant and out of control. For years I'd used porn to help me get to sleep. After an hour or so of watching porn, I could hit the sleep button and have a good 2-3 hours kip on an afternoon when I got home from training or work. But something strange was happening. From the day I said that prayer, I would try to go to sleep after watching porn, but I would lie in bed, racked with feelings of guilt and shame. I just couldn't get to sleep as I used to and I didn't understand why. This feeling was new to me. I also felt an urge to take much more of an interest in the things of God. I started watching a lot of pastors and preachers on the GOD TV channel. I would listen intently to what they were teaching and saying. I found a few specific people I liked listening to and found their messages extremely profound! It all made sense; almost like my eyes were being opened to the truth of life. I didn't know this at the time, but I discovered later that in the Bible it's written,

> *"Consequently, faith comes from hearing the message, and the message is heard through the Word about Christ"*

God was revealing to me truths that psychologists claimed were new discoveries but were in fact written about in the Bible over 2000 years ago. For example, I'd watched a documentary some years before about people who try to break bad habits, but often struggle to quit them because they are constantly thinking about that particular thing they are trying to stop which makes them want to do it more. Then amazingly, I found out the apostle Paul, who wrote three-quarters of the New Testament, had written in Romans 7:14-25,

> *"I don't really understand myself, for I want to do what is right, but I don't do it. Instead, I do what I hate…… I have discovered this principle of life—that when I want to do what is right, I inevitably do what is wrong. I love God's law with all my heart. But there is another power within me that is at war with my mind. This power makes me a slave to the sin that is still within me. Oh, what a miserable person I am! Who will free me from this life that is dominated by sin and death? Thank God! The answer is in Jesus Christ our Lord. So, you see how it is: In my mind I really want to obey God's law, but because of my sinful nature I am a slave to sin"*

Wow! This passage could have been me talking about my own life. I felt exactly like this! I felt like a slave to porn and sex and it was dominating me! I knew I needed to stop watching porn. God was showing me, through a new understanding that I was discovering, just how harmful pornography was and how it had warped my mind from the age of eleven. I looked at almost every woman as a sexual object and not as a valuable person with feelings and emotions. It had affected my whole relational life and I'd had enough! But it wasn't going to be as straightforward as I thought.

Rugby Career Ends

Meanwhile, the 2009 rugby season was ending. At Featherstone we finished in sixth place in the Championship, making the play-offs. We'd had a bit of an up and down season. On a personal note, I'd established myself back in the team after my bicep operation and I had been playing reasonably well. But to be honest, by my own high standards, I was disappointed. I wasn't enjoying it as much and some of that was down to my job as a postman. Although the hours fitted in well with my rugby, I hadn't anticipated just how physical a job it was going to be. I was walking over ten miles a day, carrying up to six or seven heavy mail bags throughout my round. It wasn't the best occupation to combine with playing professional rugby. During matches, I had less energy and felt less dynamic. The coach at the time, Daryl Powell, was trying to instil a more professional full-time environment at the club. He changed the training schedule dramatically when he first arrived at the club. I could see what he was trying to achieve but it was always going to be a stretch with a part-time playing squad. Daryl decided to bring the players in early in the mornings to do a forty-five-minute weights session. Then they would go to work all day and come back in the evening to do a field session for two hours. I thought this was too much of a burden on part-time players. Many had young families so weren't seeing their wives and children at all some days. It certainly bred some resentment in the team and Daryl wasn't popular at all with some of the players. He also changed the last session before a game from a Friday evening to a Saturday morning. I only got one Saturday off every six weeks at Royal Mail, so I explained to him that it wouldn't be possible for me to attend those Saturday sessions. Daryl had little sympathy and simply told me that if I didn't train on a Saturday, then he wouldn't select me to play. It felt harsh, but I understood that if he allowed me that concession, then other players would want it too. So, I made the decision to do something that would have got me sacked from my job at Royal Mail if they ever found out. I would go into work at the delivery office on a Saturday morning, load up my car with mail, and then jet off to Featherstone to train. Then immediately after the training session I would go back and finish off my round. I wasn't getting finished until 4 pm on a Saturday afternoon and I was shattered. Not ideal preparation for a game. Plus, if I had got caught with mail in my car outside of my delivery area, I would have been instantly sacked and investigated for theft of mail. But I made the choice to do what I had to do to keep my place in the team.

We had a great run in the playoffs that season. We beat Sheffield Eagles away in a humdinger of a match! Our captain Iestyn Harris came up with an unusual plan to start a fight in the first tackle of the game to upset their big forward pack. We won the toss which allowed us to kick off to them. Funnily enough, it was Iestyn who made that first tackle of the game. And true to his word, when the Sheffield player stood up to play the ball, Iestyn started swinging punches and laying into their player. And sticking to the script, the rest of us were ready on our toes and raced in to create an all-out brawl! It was like something out of the WWE Royal Rumble! But the plan certainly worked, and it got us all fired up too. We got away with it, as we knew the referee would have to have some big balls to send anyone off in the first minute of such an important play-off match. We went on to beat Widnes away in the next playoff game which was another upset and a fantastic win. We found ourselves just eighty minutes away from reaching a Grand Final and we travelled to Halifax in the semi-final. It ended up in a cruel 32-30 loss which would turn out to be my last ever game of rugby league. As I suspected would happen, the club didn't offer me another contract at the end of that season. I decided to tentatively look for another club. I was 27 years old, and technically, I should have been entering the peak of my playing career. But the offers I received weren't incredibly attractive. This, combined with me becoming disillusioned with the sport I once loved, accumulated in me deciding to call time on my rugby career. I'd long ago stopped enjoying the sport. I'd reached the highest level of the sport, playing in Super League and I felt I had nothing more to prove to myself. I was done! You'd expect it to be a difficult decision to make, but surprisingly it wasn't. Many sportspeople experience what is known as 'retirement euphoria' and it was something I appeared to be experiencing. Rugby League is such a high impact physical game and you put your body through a lot of pain. I was so dedicated, and I lived and breathed the rugby game.

Through the introduction of GPS devices now built into rugby shirts, sports scientists have the ability to measure the impact of every collision. They found that on average, every tackle is the equivalent of being in a 30mph car crash. Rugby League is mentally tough too. Always knowing that if you don't go out and perform to the best of your ability every week, you can easily find yourself looking for another occupation in a very short time. Also, players don't get paid a fortune either, so they know they will have to find another source of income after they've retired from playing.

Ultimately, I embraced retirement, and me and Josie booked a two-week Caribbean cruise. I was so excited to spend some quality time on holiday, especially with Roxy. She was still only two and a half years old, but I wanted to make it as memorable for her as my holidays were when I was a kid. Not long after that holiday, Josie fell pregnant again. I was happy that Roxy wouldn't be an only child, as I'd loved growing up with a brother. I also applied for a different job, but still within Royal Mail. I applied for a full-time driving job in Specialist Services, which I desperately needed now I'd retired from professional rugby. Fortunately, I got the job, but the hours weren't ideal. I started work at 4 am in the morning and finished at 2 pm in the afternoon, which meant I was getting up at 3 am for six days of the week. However, I was about to meet someone who would take my life on a new path......

Chapter 9
Trials And Tribulations

My new job at Royal Mail started soon after I got back from our holiday. To begin with, I enjoyed the novelty of a new job and not having the pressure of being a professional rugby player. And to be honest, the job didn't require much brainpower. It was more of a manual labour job. I was driving about 200 miles a day in a 3.5-tonne van delivering sensitive mail to banks and building societies in the vicinity of Yorkshire, so I was out and about all day, which I really enjoyed. I'd moved workplace to the Royal Mail Centre Headquarters in Leeds. One of the perks of the job was that I got to use the Royal Mail centre's gymnasium for a discounted price. It allowed me to train and maintain a good level of fitness that I'd built up during my rugby career. I would usually do a session after my shift had finished. After a few months, I noticed a stunning woman training in the gym named Melanie. Mel also worked at Royal Mail in the sales department and helped on the gym committee board. I won't lie, I was instantly attracted to Mel. She was a stunning black woman. At the risk of sounding cheesy, she had the looks and figure of exactly how I would have described my dream woman. I tried to be cool and collected around her, but I was very much in awe of her beauty. There was certainly some chemistry between us, and I got the sense that she had a lovely soul. She lit up the room when she came in and she had a bubbly, infectious personality. It wasn't long before we exchanged numbers and started messaging each other. Mel was single and had a two-year-old boy named Zac. So that was one thing we had in common from the start. Initially, I didn't disclose my situation at home to Mel, for the fear that she'd run a mile. We arranged to meet up outside of work and we began a physical relationship. I knew what I was doing was wrong, but I'd been behaving this way since I was seventeen years old. I was well-practised at covering my tracks. I soon came clean to Mel about my situation at home, which of course she was upset about. But I knew she liked me, and I think she could feel there was a real connection between us. Something that really struck me about Mel was that she was such a positive and encouraging person. For example, we'd not known each other long when we were in Leeds city centre together one day. We passed a lady and Mel suddenly grabbed her attention and said, *"Wow, your shoes look great on you! Where did you get them from?"* Now, this might seem strange when I say this, but I was bowled over by her comment! I had been so used to being in a situation with Josie, where she would see another female who was looking good, and rather than compliment her, she would say something negative about her, in a kind of jealous and insecure way. Over the time I'd been with Josie, I'd started to believe that all women were like that. But Mel showed me in this one moment that this wasn't true and that made me even more attracted to her. Mel also struck me as being a strong, ambitious woman, which I also found to be a very attractive quality.

However, mentally I was in turmoil! I couldn't concentrate and I was encountering so many different emotions, one of which was deep guilt. I had a partner who was pregnant, and I had a three-year-old daughter at home. I felt I had to tell someone just to try and relieve the pressure. So, I decided to speak to my mum. I'd always been close to my mum and she was a very understanding person. It was so grim to break this news to her and I could visibly see how disappointed she was. Fortunately, she understood and initially, I felt better for telling her. The only problem was, she told my dad. My dad arranged to meet up with me in private. I knew what was coming and during our chat, he told me in no uncertain terms what an idiot I would be if I was to throw away everything I had. I guess he was right to a certain degree and it was what I expected him to say. In June of 2010, me, Josie, and Roxy went on a summer holiday to Cornwall. It had been arranged for months. I was struggling to cope with the stress and guilt, but I tried to make the most of a week away with Roxy. She was always great fun to be around and I loved her immensely. From the moment she was born, I loved being a dad to her! But that week away was confirmation that I no longer wanted to be with Josie. The double life I was living had become unbearable. I was growing closer to Mel and I was finding it increasingly difficult to be away from her. But I was still in a massive quandary. I knew that if I came clean to Josie about my relationship with Mel, then that would shatter her world! But my biggest concern was how it would affect Roxy. I loved being a hands-on dad and I knew this would change if I split up with Josie. I wasn't sure how I would cope with not seeing Roxy every day. And I knew the fallout in the family would be treacherous. Everyone would know just what a heartless individual I was, to do that to my pregnant partner! I was certain I would be harshly judged for my actions.

Turmoil

A few days after our week away in Cornwall, I sat down with Josie and came clean about me seeing Mel. I explained to her that I was no longer in love with her and that I wanted to split up. It was the most agonising thing I've ever had to do in my life. To say she was devastated is an understatement. As soon as I told her, she was inconsolable, and she began to vomit. It was like watching a film when people receive the news that a loved one has tragically died. What could I do? I had nothing but sorrow, guilt, and shame for the pain I had caused her. No amount of apologising could make it any better. I was also concerned about our unborn daughter as well. How would this physical and mental trauma affect the baby? Soon after I broke the news to Josie, she took off with Roxy and went over to my mum and dad's house to give them the news. Although it was tough,

I did feel some relief that I had now come clean, but things weren't going to be easy in the following weeks and months. It was the most trying and testing time of my life. The fallout within the family from my actions was huge. The next month or so, while we still lived together was a strange time. Josie would often beg me not to leave her, then at other times, she would be angry at me again. I just didn't want to be around her. I tried my best to help her practically. Within a couple of months, Josie had found a nice rental property close to her mum and dad's home in the south of Leeds. Her new house was unfurnished, so I bought her everything she needed, such as a sofa, TV, fridge, freezer, washer, dryer, etc. Some would say that I was just doing it out of guilt. And yes, I felt an enormous amount of guilt and shame for how things had turned out, but I genuinely wanted her, Roxy, and my unborn child to have a good, quality, comfortable place to live. I spent over three thousand pounds on items for her new house, although I knew whatever I did for her, it was never going to be enough to heal the pain I'd caused. I was getting plenty of grief from Josie's family too. Her sister sent me some abusive text messages and I was thrown a barrage of verbal abuse when I crossed paths with Josie's mum while I was helping Josie move into her new house. But I couldn't really blame any of them; they were simply sticking up for their own flesh and blood. Josie moved in with Roxy about a month before she was due to give birth. I'd hoped she would be reasonable about me having access to Roxy. But this proved to be wishful thinking.

My new-born daughter, Anna, was born on 5 September 2010. Josie didn't want me anywhere near her for the birth which I could understand. I was sad about that though because it felt amazing being at Roxy's birth. I was happy when Anna was born, and I felt a massive sigh of relief that Anna was a healthy new-born. I was so thankful to God as I'd prayed for Anna's health. I knew the emotional trauma that Josie had been going through could have affected Anna in some way or another. I first got a chance to hold Anna at my parents' house a couple of days after she was born.

Again, the overwhelming feeling of love for her hit me like a train! From that moment, I fell in love with Anna. But things were not going to be as straightforward as I'd hoped. As you can imagine, there was a lot of bitterness and resentment from Josie towards both me and Mel. I tried to offer as much support as I could for Josie. I just wanted to be a stable part of Roxy and Anna's life. However, Josie began to prevent me from seeing both Roxy and Anna. I fully understood that she would want to spend time with Anna and to bond with her during those early months. But I also wanted time to bond with her as her father. In the end, she allowed me to see Roxy once a week, but not Anna. Even that statement, *"She allowed me to see Roxy"*, is so wrong. No parent should be able to have more control than another. But this was under the strict condition that Mel wouldn't be there when I had Roxy. I certainly was not happy at only having Roxy once a week. I'd gone from being with her every day and playing a major part in her upbringing to only seeing her once a week. I certainly did not want to be that type of dad. I attempted to reason with Josie, and I explored the option of us coming up with a plan that enabled me to have access to Roxy and Anna, and that Josie felt happy to consent to. I saw no reason why we couldn't split the time 50/50 between us both. But Josie was having none of this and during a conversation, she said, *"I am not agreeing to anything unless it's in court!"* Initially, I was taken aback by her response! I tried to explain to her that this would mean that someone else (a judge,) would decide for us how we would split the time we spent with our daughters. I couldn't understand why on earth she would want this. I suspected that some of her friends and family had been influencing her decisions. She left me with no choice, and I sought legal advice to see where I stood on child arrangement matters. I was advised that fathers have the same rights as mothers and that because I had been such a major part of Roxy's life to date, then it should be a straightforward court application. Consequently, I made an application to the family courts for a contact order, but things were not going to be plain sailing.

God Speaks

As me and Mel got to know each better, I plucked up the courage to talk to Mel about my faith in God. I was apprehensive at first, given Josie's negative response to anything about God or Jesus. But amazingly, Mel was really interested in my faith. She asked loads of questions and we talked for hours. Her overall response was really encouraging to me and I immediately felt comfortable expressing myself in Mel's presence. We had only known each other for just over six months now but our relationship was already so much deeper than anything I had ever experienced before. Me and Mel talked all night about God. We shared a similar spiritual view of life. Mel was fascinated when I explained to her what the Bible had to say about the end times and how Jesus was coming back. I think it helped that she had been brought up going to church with her family as a young girl. But she also felt like me, in the way she found the whole church experience quite dull and boring. Tommy had told me about a church in Bradford called Abundant Life Church. Tommy told me how it was a very modern church that was 'spiritually alive'. I also knew an old teammate of mine I'd played with at Wakefield called Semi Tadulala. He was a Fijian born player who had recently become born again and started going to this church. I mentioned it to Mel, and she was really keen to check it out. We went along one Sunday evening and we were utterly blown away from the moment we arrived. It was worlds apart from the church experiences I'd had growing up when attending weddings, christenings, and funerals. It was a very modern-looking building and there wasn't a statue of Mary or Jesus in sight. They even had car parking attendants with glow sticks directing us where to park. I was instantly intrigued. The first 30 minutes of the service was like a pop concert. There was a full band on a massive stage playing loud, upbeat, and inspiring music. People were singing their hearts out, worshipping God with their hands in the air. The size of the place was unbelievable; there must have been nearly two thousand people in there. I'd never seen anything like this in a church before! The people seemed so happy too. I remember thinking, *"Now, this is how church should be!"* The message from the pastor was amazing too. It was like he knew the situation I was going through with Josie and the girls and it felt like he was talking directly to me. He was talking about 'fighting the good fight' and his whole message resonated with me about fighting to be a father to Roxy and Anna. It was so inspiring and encouraging, it blew me sideways! I knew Mel was enjoying it too and as we walked out after the service, she turned to me and gasped, *"That was like he was talking to you then!"* I replied with, *"I'm glad you said that because that's exactly how I felt."*

Could God have been speaking to me through the pastor's message? We started to attend every Sunday and we both began to grow in our faith and gained inspiration through the whole church experience.

Freedom

Around this time, I decided that I was going to stop watching porn. I had a massive revelation moment when God actually showed me, through my own family, just how and why this addiction had taken such a grip on me. I started to think about my Uncle Mick, who was my mum's twin brother. He had gone through his whole life as a serial womaniser. He always seemed like he couldn't help himself. He would always end up being unfaithful to his wife or partner. It was a familiar pattern throughout his whole life even into his fifties. I recognised that my own life had followed this same pattern. I also recalled my maternal grandad explaining to me how he always had an eye for the ladies and that he had been caught having an affair with the woman who lived next door to them. My grandma even found out but, in those days, a couple rarely split up. I think he had other affairs too. Then, I discovered that in the Old Testament, in the book of Exodus, chapter 34, God says, *"I lay the sins of the parents upon their children; the entire family is affected—even children in the third and fourth generations of those who reject me"*.

This type of sin had affected my family for generations and now it was affecting me, just like God says in this verse. God was opening my eyes and showing me there was a spiritual reason why I was the way I was. This passage in the book of Ephesians 2, explained me to me perfectly,

"Once you were dead because of your disobedience and your many sins. You used to live in sin, just like the rest of the world, obeying the devil—the commander of the powers in the unseen world. He is the spirit at work in the hearts of those who refuse to obey God. All of us used to live that way, following the passionate desires and inclinations of our sinful nature. By our very nature we were subject to God's anger, just like everyone else"

I learned that the word 'sin' simply means to fall short of God's best. It all made total sense. I was born into this sin tendency and that's why the sexual sin was affecting me so deeply. It felt so much like it was a part of me because it was! But now I was born again! I had the Holy Spirit living on the inside of me and I could choose to follow God's Way.

The world wants us to believe it is fine to watch porn and that it is harmless fun. But God's Word is noticeably clear on this. In 1 John 2:16 it is written, *"For everything in the world—the lust of the flesh, the lust of the eyes, and the pride of life—comes not from the Father but from the world"*.

There is no doubt that pornography causes us to lust after flesh, and it is undeniably a *"lust of the eyes"*. Jesus famously said in Matthew 5, *"You have heard that it was said, 'You shall not commit adultery'. But I tell you that anyone who looks at a woman lustfully has already committed adultery with her in his heart"*.

Watching porn certainly causes us to look lustfully at people.

I'd achieved so much in my life to date, particularly in my sporting career. I'd done most of it all through determination and will power.

So, stopping watching porn was going to be easy, or so I thought. I tried so hard to stop, but time and time again, the urge was there to watch it and I did. I felt like a failure. But I'd heard messages on GOD TV about how God was so powerful and all you had to do was ask God for what you needed. I decided to be bold and ask God to help me stop watching porn. My prayer went a bit like this, *"Dear Lord, I've tried so hard to stop watching porn, but I can't do it! Please God, will you help me stop?"*

It was a simple prayer really and I was trying to be honest and vulnerable with God. As the following weeks passed by, I noticed that I'd not watched porn since I'd said that prayer. Maybe God *was* helping me? Then, before I knew it, I didn't even want to watch porn anymore. I started to view women differently too and I no longer felt the fleshly urges I had felt before. In its own way, it was a total miracle! This thing that had controlled me for so long, seemingly no longer had a hold on me!

Interestingly, Paul says in 2 Corinthians 5:17, *"At one time we thought of Christ merely from a human point of view. How differently we know him now! This means that anyone who belongs to Christ has become a new person. The old life is gone; a new life has begun!"*

Wow! I was experiencing this Biblical truth in my life. I felt like the old me had gone and God was transforming me into a new person from the inside out! This passage in Galatians 5 also explained to me what was happening, *"So I say, let the Holy Spirit guide your lives. Then you won't be doing what your sinful nature craves. The sinful nature wants to do evil, which is just the opposite of what the Spirit wants. And the Spirit gives us desires that are the opposite of what the sinful nature desires. These two forces are constantly fighting each other, so you are not free to carry out your good intentions. But when you are directed by the Spirit, you are not under obligation to the law of Moses".*

By allowing my life to be guided by the Holy Spirit that dwelt in me, from the moment I invited Jesus into my heart, I was experiencing real freedom. I'd initially thought nothing had happened when I invited Jesus in, but it had! It was a massive turning point in my life, but with all the fallout from my past behaviour, I was about to experience betrayal by my own family on a level I could have never imagined……

Chapter 10
Court Battle Number 1

The decision to take Josie to court wasn't difficult, given the fact she was already making it virtually impossible for me to see Roxy and Anna. As my relationship with Mel was becoming more serious, I sensed that Josie would make any contact even more problematic. All I wanted was a stable routine for Roxy and Anna so they could maintain a good relationship with both me and their mum. But things took a sinister turn when Josie got the court papers through, about my application to take her to court. Her attitude towards me completely turned and she became very hostile towards both me and Mel. At first, she started messing about with contact arrangements we'd made, then she started to make up false allegations to the police every week. The police came over to my house and threatened me with a harassment order for ringing and messaging her. Josie also started reporting Mel to the police for all manner of things that were totally made up. She was on a mission and it was relentless! The police would ring either me or Mel to ask us about whatever allegation Josie had made up that week. There was one occasion Josie claimed that Mel had gone over to her house and made violent threats to her. What was crazy about this allegation, was that we were actually at church when Josie claimed this happened. I think the police must have thought that was the perfect alibi. But it was true and plenty of people could testify to our whereabouts. This went on for months! Mel was even the target of racial abuse from Josie and her cousin on social media. We'd seen some nasty comments on Facebook, directed at Mel. Josie's cousin had tried to use the abbreviation "BB" in a Facebook post which meant 'black bitch'. I knew her cousin and her family well from my time with Josie, so I knew what they could be like and their comments didn't really surprise me. They are the type of people who are happy to hide behind a screen but wouldn't dare say anything to your face. To be fair to the police, when we explained our situation, they were sympathetic to us. They explained to us that this was the type of thing they had to deal with regularly, especially in these circumstances where court proceedings are pending. They told us that they were fully aware of Josie trying to use the police in order to strengthen her case. I think Josie's first agenda was to try and land me or Mel with a criminal record so she could use this in court, in order to stop us from having the girls. But also, I think she was attempting to make life so difficult for Mel that it would cause fractions in our relationship. But in fact, all Josie achieved by her actions was to push me and Mel even closer together as a couple. All the adversity we were dealing with, helped to forge our relationship even stronger. I'd started to lose any respect I had left for Josie. Sadly, she had turned very bitter and resentful! We have all heard the saying, "A woman scorned!" She seemed prepared to do anything to gain revenge, including using Roxy and Anna as weapons to hurt me. I knew it was a typical response from some women in this situation, but that didn't make it right. There's a true but sad saying, 'hurt people, hurt people' and this was certainly the case with Josie.

Family Betrayal

What I hadn't bargained for though, was my own family turning their back on me. My dad would call me up and berate me for taking Josie to court. He would tell me that I was out of order and that I was wasting my money. He tried to convince me that the courts always side with the mother. My parents were also regularly inviting Josie around to their house for tea. I felt so betrayed by their actions. I couldn't understand why they were being so disloyal. Josie was preventing me from seeing my daughters and was forcing me to spend loads of money to take her to court just so I could be a father to them. She was making mine and Mel's lives extremely difficult by making up so many false allegations to the police in order to get us a criminal record. All the while, my parents were behaving like they were best friends with her. I realise I'd not been a perfect son to them, but I expected some loyalty. But I also knew that Josie was doing a great job of making everybody sympathise with her. It wasn't difficult, given the fact I'd left her for another woman while she was six months pregnant. Don't get me wrong, I didn't want any sympathy from anyone, but I did expect some support from my own family.

My brother also rubbed salt in this wound when he and his wife arranged a Halloween party at their house. He invited our whole family along with Josie, but I wasn't invited. I just couldn't believe what was going on! I felt hurt and betrayed. Josie took great delight in telling me that she'd been invited and that I was no longer having Roxy and Anna that night, as had been previously arranged. I made the decision to go over to my brother's house to collect Roxy and Anna that evening, as had been initially arranged. When I arrived at his house, everyone was in fancy dress and I could feel the atmosphere shift as I entered. I certainly didn't feel welcome. My whole family was sat around playing happy families with Josie, laughing, and joking. It made me feel sick to my stomach. But I remained calm and collected. After exchanging pleasantries with my extended family, I explained to Josie that I'd come to collect Roxy and Anna. At this point, Josie started crying and playing the victim. My mum took sympathy on her and took Josie, Roxy, and Anna in her car and drove them home. Josie had played a blinder; I'd been left to look like the villain for coming to collect my daughters as had been originally arranged. The events of this night confirmed to me how Josie had the same manipulative personality traits as I'd witnessed in her mum. A few days following that night, my brother apologised to me and admitted that he was wrong to invite Josie and exclude me. I respected him more for being humble enough to admit he was wrong. It was around this time that me and Mel arranged to stay at my parent's caravan in Scarborough for a few days. However, my mum later told me that we couldn't go because Josie was going that same weekend with her cousin. Again, it was relentless, and my family was blind to Josie's games, but things were about to become even more dreadful before they got better.

When my dad discovered that Mel was a black woman and that she had a little boy, he was very angry, and he let me know his distaste. Although I was fully aware of his racist views, I'd hoped that by now, his opinions had matured. But I was wrong. He phoned me and during our conversation, he told me, *"The last thing me and your mum want is a mixed-race grandchild!"*

They were his very words and I was dumbfounded by what he'd just said! There was no excuse for his racist comment. A few days later I went over to my parents' house and confronted him about what he'd said. I made it clear that what he'd said was blatantly racist and out of order, but he tried to excuse himself by pleading that he was in no way a racist. But I knew his heart. God's Word even says, *"For the mouth speaks what the heart is full of"* Matthew 12:34. And it's so true when people are angry or under stress, what is truly in their heart comes out in their words. I didn't dare tell Mel what he'd said. Mel hadn't met my dad yet and I didn't want to tarnish her view of him. Plus, she was really feeling the strain of all the false allegations being made against her by Josie. This had contributed to her losing weight from the stress of it all. Mel certainly wasn't the type of person to take all these false allegations lying down. However, she was wise enough to realise that if she lashed out at Josie in any way, either physically or verbally, it would play straight into her hands. Also, as we were both now followers of Jesus, we were trying to put into practice what we were learning. Jesus said, *"But I tell you, love your enemies and pray for those who persecute you"*. But this was proving to be a challenge.

Court Battle Number 1

The first court hearing soon came around in November 2010. I was sad that it had come to this, but it was the only option I'd been left with if I wanted to be a father to Roxy and Anna. Roxy was three years old; Anna was only two months old and Zac had just turned three. I had a solicitor representing me who I was paying for privately and Josie had a solicitor who was funded by the government as she was on a low income. It seemed quite unfair that she could have a lawyer free of charge in order to prevent me from seeing my children. But that was just how the system worked then and there was nothing I could do about it. The court hearing was listed at Leeds County Court in front of District Judge Jordan. Josie's solicitor spoke first and as I expected, she attempted to make me out to be some scumbag individual. I was itching for my solicitor to put her straight, but she said very little. She just stuck to the matter of the child arrangements and pretty much ignored Josie's solicitor. A Children and Family Court Advisory and Support Service Officer (CAFCASS) was at the hearing. They basically act as social services representatives for the court. The judge asked the CAFCASS officer if there were any safeguarding concerns about either parent. This is where I was expecting her to bring up all the false allegations Josie had made about me and Mel. The officer said, *"There are no specific safeguarding concerns, but…"*. Then District Judge Jordan abruptly cut her off and said, *"Thank you, please leave the courtroom as we don't need you in this case anymore"*. I've no doubt that the CAFCASS officer was about to reel off the list of allegations that had been made by Josie, but I think the judge had seen it all before and didn't even begin to entertain it. I could see by the look on Josie and her solicitors' faces that they were gutted by this. This was their only ammunition and it had been taken away. The judge encouraged us to agree on some interim contact before the next hearing, which was due to take place in six weeks. I managed to get Roxy for one day during the week and one overnight stay on a weekend. As for Anna, Josie insisted that I see her for an hour at a time at her house. Josie pleaded that she didn't want Anna to be away from her while she was still so young. I agreed to go along

Court Battle Number 1

with this. Josie was also making a big deal about Mel being there, while I had Roxy. She was saying it was because it was a new relationship, but I knew she would never be happy with Mel being there. I felt like I was being controlled by Josie, but on the advice of my solicitor, I went along with it to show understanding and compromise to the court.

I quickly learned that the family court is very much what is referred to as a 'Mickey Mouse' court. It's vastly different from a criminal court. In a family court, allegations are taken as fact without any proof needed. The judge essentially acts as a referee and prefers both parents to agree on how the contact is to be shared. This can then be put into what's known as a 'consented order'. But ultimately, if contact cannot be agreed upon, then the case gets listed for a 'contested Hearing'. Evidence then gets put forward by both parties to be considered by the judge, who then makes an order. If either party ever breaches the order in place, they can be punished by way of a fine, community service, or even a prison sentence. But the reality is, these orders are very rarely enforced by the court, especially if a mother breaches an order. This renders the court orders useless and not worth the paper they are written on. The problem is that many mothers are fully aware of this, so breach them regularly knowing that they will unlikely be punished.

The next hearing soon came around and I was hoping that I could increase the contact I had with both Roxy and Anna. We agreed that I could have Anna at the same time as Roxy, but Josie was still adamant that Mel could not be present when I had the girls. This seemed utterly ridiculous that she was able to still control me like this. But again, under the advice of my solicitor, I agreed to the condition. By now, I was quickly running out of money to pay my solicitor. After I'd used most of my savings to pay for all Josie's stuff for her house, I had about five thousand pounds left in savings. My solicitor's bill had now reached over six thousand pounds and I simply could not afford to be represented anymore. Solicitors aren't cheap per hourly rate which was one hundred and fifty pounds an hour. Sometimes, we would be in court all day, so my legal bill was quickly racking up! I was learning that the family court process was long, tedious, and expensive. I felt I was left with no choice, and after the second hearing, I had to go it alone and represent myself for the remainder of the court proceedings.

During this period, my mum would come over to my house to see Roxy and Anna when I had them. Relations were still strained between me and my mum with everything that had been going on, but I always felt that she was just trying to appease both sides in all this. It was not in her nature to be malicious. However, her inability to 'nail her colours to the mast' was to prove disastrous for our relationship. In January 2011, it was my mums' 54th birthday, so Mel went over to my parents' house with Zac, who was now three years old, to give my mum a birthday present. I didn't go as I'd taken Roxy to the theatre to watch a pantomime. Mel had met my mum several times, but this was the first time she'd been to my parents' house. It was also the first time Mel had met my dad. It would also prove to be the last time she would ever see my dad too. Things were about to blow up in a big way! As my mum went into the kitchen to make a cup of tea, Mel and Zac were in the living room with my dad. Mel could tell by my dad's body language that it was clear he was not happy to see her. He proceeded to give her his opinion of the whole situation. He told her that she should have stayed in the shadows for a period to make it appear that we had not been seeing each other. Then when Mel dared to question his opinion, he began an all-out verbal assault! My mum was caught in the crossfire and was embarrassed by my dad's behaviour. The first thing I knew about it was when I was leaving the theatre while carrying Roxy on my shoulders. I received a phone call from Mel who was clearly upset by what had just happened. As I've mentioned before Mel is a strong, independent woman who doesn't suffer fools, so I knew something serious had occurred. She went on to tell me what had happened at my parents' house and the way my dad had spoken to

Court Battle Number 1

her. I was furious! But at least Mel had experienced first-hand what my dad could be like. For me, this was the straw that broke the camel's back! I called my dad the very next day and told him that he had yet again overstepped the mark! I told him I no longer wanted anything to do with him. I think he was shocked, but I was serious and meant every word. After this incident, my mum would continue to visit my house most weeks to see me and the girls, but my dad was obviously not welcome. My mum had told me that when she would return home from visiting me, my dad would make her feel guilty for coming to see me and the kids. You see, my dad had always tended to be passive-aggressive. My mum also told me how he would do the same thing if she didn't want to go to the caravan on a weekend. Because he always wanted to go, he would make my mum's weekend miserable, by giving her the silent treatment and creating a bad atmosphere. It's a very subtle form of control which I began to recognise and understand.

As the next court hearing came around in February 2011, I was feeling nervous about representing myself. Mel offered to come along to support me. I was glad to have her support and she knew how important Roxy and Anna were to me although I knew she would not be allowed in the courtroom itself. The family courts are private and are known as secret courts. This can bring a lot of criticism, as the judges and CAFCASS officers are not made accountable for the decisions they make. It's a terrible system when you think about it. As we walked into the court waiting area and sat down, Josie and her friend were sitting opposite us. Josie's friend made a snide comment to Mel. Mel stood up to confront her about what she'd just said. Josie and her friend both stood up, so Mel ended up being face to face with them both, as a verbal argument broke out. Mel let Josie know exactly what she thought about her cowardly attempts to tarnish her name. Things soon calmed down, as Josie and her friend walked away to sit somewhere else. Then after about 15 minutes, two police officers came into the court and approached Mel. They asked her to confirm her name and proceeded to arrest her on the spot, on suspicion of assault. They explained that Josie had accused Mel of punching and spitting at her. I couldn't believe what was going on! I'd been a witness to exactly what had happened, and Mel hadn't done anything wrong. In fact, she showed a substantial amount of restraint, considering what she'd had to deal with. The court hearing went ahead but as I expected, Josie and her solicitor made a big deal of Mel being arrested. Ultimately, there wasn't a great deal of progress made at this hearing, which was very frustrating. But Josie was happy as it enabled her to drag out the case for longer and she likely believed that she'd succeeded in smearing Mel's reputation. The judge set a date for the next hearing, by which time we'd know the outcome of Mel's arrest. To my shock, Mel was banged up in a police cell for over six hours. She phoned me when she was released, and I went to collect her. The police had viewed the CCTV in the court waiting area which clearly showed that Mel had done nothing wrong and that Josie had fabricated the whole incident. The adversity of this incident simply served to strengthen mine and Mel's resolve. It brought us even closer together as a couple and we knew we had each other's back. As it says in Romans 8:28, *"God works all things together for good, for those who love God and are called according to his purpose for them"*, although I was astonished that someone was able to make so many false allegations and waste police time with no consequences! And what hurts me even more, was that my own family were supporting Josie's actions. This incident turned out to be the catalyst for me to confront my family about their support of her.

Defiance

I'd had enough of Josie's cowardly antics and I was also at my wits end about my own family's lack of loyalty. Even after all that had happened, my parents, grandparents, and my brother were still welcoming of Josie and she had a very cosy relationship with my parents. I decided to speak to my mum, my brother, and my grandad about it. After explaining my hurt and disappointment of their disloyalty, I gave them an ultimatum, *"It's either me or her, you choose!"* It was as simple as that. My brother was sympathetic and agreed with what I was asking. However, my grandad was not so understanding and made it clear that he would not choose. My mum said, *"Of course I'm going to choose my own son"*. Mel asked me at the time if I thought my mum would stick to her word. I said, *"Out of anyone I know, the one person I can trust is my mum!"*.

However, about six weeks later, I found out that my mum had been to Josie's house with my dad. I felt utterly crushed! I rang my mum up to find out if it was true. My mum confirmed to me that it was true. During our short conversation, I told my mum how she had broken my trust and I felt our relationship was over. It was a tough conversation to have because you only get one mum, but I had to stick by my convictions. Also, I suspected that my dad had twisted her arm, in order to get her to go with him to Josie's house. But my mum had her own mind and she was more than capable of making her own decisions. I had now effectively cut off all contact with both my mum, dad, and grandparents.

The next court hearing came around at the start of April 2011. Roxy was now four years old; Zac was three and Anna was seven months old. Me and Mel had known each other for almost a year now. But Josie was still demanding that Mel couldn't be present when I had Roxy and Anna. Josie and her solicitor tried their hardest to make Mel out to be some violent thug, even though Josie had been ousted for making up false allegations at the previous hearing. Thankfully, District Judge Jordan was having none of it and he dismissed her demands. Plus, me and Mel had recently moved in together. It was so obvious how controlling Josie was being. She was also digging in her heels on various aspects of the contact. She wanted to have Roxy and Anna overnight, every Christmas Eve. I felt it was fair to share these out and have them on alternate Christmas Eve's. The Judge agreed with my proposal. He turned to Josie and sternly said, *"If you cause this case to go to a contested hearing because you dig your heels in on this issue, I can assure you that I will be the judge in the contested hearing and I will rule in dad's favour"*. Brilliant, I could have kissed him! He also explained to us that in Scandinavia, when parents split up, contact begins with 50/50 shared care and he believed it should be the same in this country. That makes total sense to me and it is one of the reasons why Scandinavian countries are so advanced in many social aspects.

So, we managed to agree on a consented contact order which I was happy with. We would have Roxy and Anna on alternate weekends, Friday to Sunday. One week, we would have them on a Tuesday and a Thursday. The following week, we would have them on a Tuesday. But because of the hours I worked at Royal Mail at the time, I was unable to have them overnight during the week, which was a shame, so I would drop them back off at their mum's at 8 pm. I managed to get plenty of holiday time put in the order too. We could have them for two separate weeks in the summer school holiday, one of the weeks we could take them abroad. I wanted two weeks abroad, but Josie dug her heels in on this. We had arrangements for the Easter, February, and October half terms too. This court order would ultimately prove crucial to maintaining a stable routine for Roxy and Anna, but also us as a family. The whole court thing was a massive weight off my shoulders. The process had been unnecessarily long and drawn out, but it was worth it in the end. I had a huge sense of pride that I'd 'fought the good fight' for Roxy and Anna. Me, Mel, Roxy, Zac, and Anna could now be free to get on with being a family. Me and Mel were so happy together and I was super excited about our future as a family. But not everything was going to be as straightforward as I'd expected it to be……

Chapter 11
Nurturing A Blended Family

For the past eight months, Mel had been wise enough to keep her composure and stay calm while Josie was having free rein to harass her and make vicious attempts to slander her character in so many different ways. Although it had caused Mel an intense amount of stress, I was so proud of the way she handled herself throughout this whole process. Many less emotionally strong people would have run a mile from our relationship. However, after all the false allegations and harassment that Mel had been subject to, she had a little surprise up her sleeve for Josie. And with the court case over, now was a perfect time. Mel knew there was more than one way to skin a cat, so she decided to go into the shop where Josie worked. It was a well-known ladies' lingerie shop. Mel went in and requested a bra fitting, which Josie was trained to do. When Josie entered the fitting room and saw it was Mel, ready to be fitted up, it totally sent her over the edge. Josie ran off crying to her boss and had to be consoled. Mel had just exposed Josie for exactly the type of person she was, a coward who when she came face to face with the person she had been tormenting for so long, simply ran away and hid. And true to form, afterwards, Josie made as much noise as she could about it. She attempted to get Mel banned from the shopping centre, which failed. So, she went a step further and even took Mel to court and attempted to get a non-molestation order against her. But once again her cowardly attempts failed. It all came to nothing as there was no substance to her claims and it was practically laughed out of court.

My beautiful family

Nurturing A Blended Family

Anna was a great baby and I adored being a dad to her just as much as I loved being a dad to Roxy. She was such a happy, contented baby who loved being around her family, especially her brother, Zac, and sister, Roxy. All three children quickly adapted to our family unit. I think it was easier for them to adjust, as they were so young. When Roxy and Zac first met each other, Roxy was three years old and Zac was two. There is just a nine-month age gap between them. They got on like a house on fire right from the start. Mel is an amazing mum and she took Roxy and Anna on like they were her own flesh and blood. I understood that with a stepchild, the natural bond is not there, but Mel quickly built up the trust of the girls and they enjoyed being with Mel. I was so proud of her and it strengthened our relationship even more. I loved being a dad to Zac too. We quickly built a close relationship. It was difficult at first because I so missed having Roxy and now Anna live with me full time. It took me many months to adjust to that. I think what helped mine and Zac's relationship to bond so well was that Mel had split from his biological father when Zac was a baby. His biological father never made an active attempt to be in his life, which I always felt was sad. But Zac was an absolute firecracker as a young kid. He was full of energy 24/7 and he never stopped bouncing around. He reminded me of Tiger from Winnie The Pooh! At first, I found it difficult to cope with as I'd been used to Roxy who was quite a laid back, placid child. But I embraced Zac's energy and he was always great fun to be around. He was a really intelligent kid too. Roxy and Zac made a music band in their bedroom called The Cheese and Broccoli Gang! This was because Roxy loved broccoli and Zac had cheese with every meal. On the weekends that we had Roxy and Anna, we would always arrange to do fun stuff such as taking them to a play gym, visiting a pottery café, taking them swimming, going on adventure walks to Ilkley Moor, or days out at the Go Ape Adventure Park. The list is endless of the fun activities we did as a family. It all really helped us to build a close-knit, blended family. Mind you, we used to get some funny looks from people when we were out and about. Imagine seeing a family like ours, we all looked so different. We had a white, blond hair, blue-eyed dad, a black mum, a pale-skinned, ginger-haired girl with freckles, a black boy, and a blond hair, blue-eyed toddler. We would walk by people and 50 metres down the road they would still be staring at us. They must have been trying to work out how on earth these two parents had managed to produce three, very different looking children. We always found the funny side and we appreciated that our family wasn't your ordinary, run of the mill family.

Mel also had this incredible way of getting me to go along with some of her crazy ideas. A bit like Del boy used to do with Rodney in the famous comedy series, Only Fools and Horses. She wanted to get a pet for the kids and had this quirky idea of getting a duck. That's right, a duck! How she managed to convince me, I will never know! But we ended up with a pet duck named 'Hoisin', who we bought as a baby chick. The kids loved it, but it would make a right mess of our back patio! It pooed everywhere and I was quite glad when one day, we returned home to find it had been stolen. Then Mel convinced me to get a rabbit, which we named Prinny. Again, the kids loved it! Anna was a toddler at the time, and she had this habit of grabbing at the rabbit to try and pick it up. I really could write a whole book on the happy times we've had as a family. It was the happiest I'd ever been in my life! This was partly due to us being a solid and happy family unit. But I was also experiencing freedom in my life like never before. I no longer had to lead a double life of trying to keep my porn and sex addiction covered up. It might sound like a minor thing, but not having to keep secrets or hide things from those closest to me was such a freeing experience! It made so much sense when I heard that Jesus said in John 8:36 *"So if the Son sets you free, you will be free indeed"*.

I also felt that not having my dad in my life was also a positive thing. I realised that every important decision I had made in my life, had been subconsciously affected by what I thought my dad would think about it. Maybe that says more about me than it does him, but I literally began to feel free to be exactly who God created me to be. I would even go so far as to say that I felt like a new person; born again in the literal sense. This was confirmed to me when I heard about the apostle Paul writing in 2 Corinthians 5:17, *"This means that anyone who belongs to Christ has become a new person. The old life is gone; a new life has begun!"* And I certainly felt like I was living a new life. A better, more fulfilled life. I even started to despise my old life. I was a very selfish, self-centred, womaniser and I had been simply living for my own fleshly desires. I was so grateful that God had saved me from this life!

Another Court Case

When Anna was a few months old, I applied for and obtained a passport for her. I had always dealt with these kinds of matters regarding the children, so it was natural for me to do this. However, I didn't tell Josie because I knew she would want to hold her passport and would likely kick up some drama. A matter of months after the court proceedings, Josie discovered that I had got Anna a passport when she tried to apply for one for her. As I suspected, Josie wanted to hold the passport and I received a letter from her solicitor, requesting that I hand over Anna's passport to Josie. If I didn't then they would begin court proceedings to obtain the passport. I wasn't surprised as I knew Josie's inerrant need to have control over every aspect regarding Roxy and Anna. I had no problem handing Anna's passport to Josie when she was going on holiday with her. However, I felt that as Anna's dad, with parental responsibility, why should I not be entitled to hold her passport that I had applied for. It didn't make sense. So, I stuck to my principles and Josie made a court application for Anna's passport to be forcibly removed from me, and for her to hold. I represented myself again in court as I couldn't afford any representation. I put my case forward as best I could. Unfortunately, the decision went in Josie's favour and the judge ordered that I hand Anna's passport over for her to have control of. The judge even placed an order that I will be sent to prison if I did not comply. This just proved to me that, even though fathers have equal rights in written law, when it truly came down to it, the family court was overwhelmingly biased towards mothers. The whole situation was a blatant prejudice against me as a father. The system was corrupt, but there was little I could do about it. However, during this court hearing, I did manage to get a clause added into the original contact order, that Josie must hand over the girl's passports to me, fourteen days prior to me taking them abroad. I was happy about this, as it was always a concern that Josie would try and thwart any future family holidays we had planned by not giving me the girl's passports at the last minute.

First Holiday

We went on our first holiday as a family at the end of August of 2011. We booked a static caravan on a Haven holiday site in Great Yarmouth. I was used to caravaning holidays from my time growing up, but it was all new to Mel. The first night there, we decided to go to the on-site entertainment club. It was all geared up towards children and families. I knew the standard to expect on these types of sites and that it certainly wasn't going to be the Ritz. But Mel wasn't sure what to expect. You see, Mel likes to dress very glamorously when she goes out, so she was shocked to find the other mum's out on the dance floor with their pyjama bottoms and carpet slippers on. Her face was a picture! She gave me a look as if to say, *"Where on earth have you brought me?"* I think she felt a little overdressed. But as always, we found the funny side and we embraced the week away in what was a very basic caravan. And after all, it was really for the kids and they loved the holiday. We ended up coming home a day later than expected, which turned out to be Anna's first birthday. I don't think Josie believed that we were still on holiday, so she ended up sending my dad round to our house to see if we were there. At the time, Mel's mum was at our house, as she had been feeding our rabbit. When Mel's mum answered the door, she told my dad that we were still on holiday. He then proceeded to give her a mouthful of verbal abuse which she certainly didn't deserve. I couldn't believe it! He had the gall to come round to my house on Josie's behalf! Anyway, when we got home, we had a small party for Anna. My brother came over with his kids and it was nice to celebrate her first birthday. Then we took the girls back to their mum's. However, when we got to Josie's house to drop Roxy and Anna off, she was furious! She went into a complete rage and hit me. She dragged Anna out of my arms and stormed off into the house. At the same time, a neighbour came out and shouted abuse at me. I was utterly shocked! I got back into the car with Mel and Zac and paused to think about what had just happened. Now, I've never been one for squealing to the police for minor matters, but I felt if this had been the other way round, then Josie would have used it, to make sure I never saw Roxy and Anna again. So, I decided to report what happened to the police. I also informed them about my dad coming over to my house and verbally abusing Mel's mum, even after I'd given him strict instructions never to come to my house. Josie was arrested and questioned by the police. She denied the assault and managed to get away with no charge with the help of her neighbour. Furthermore, to back up her claim that I was lying about the assault, she insisted that all future handovers should take place at the local police station. I couldn't understand why she'd want this! But I'd learned that many of her actions were for selfish reasons. Then a few days later, I received a call from the police to say that they had spoken to my dad about his behaviour. I was astounded to hear that my dad had told the police that I suffered from a form of autism called Asperger Syndrome. It was a total lie and I could only guess that he said it to try and divert any attention from his wrongdoing. But I shouldn't have been surprised that he would stoop to those kinds of tactics. In fact, it further confirmed to me that I was right to cut him out of my life. The Bible says, *"Stay away from a fool, for you will not find knowledge on their lips."*

Breaching The Order

During the weeks following Josie's arrest, Josie breached the court order on several occasions by preventing me from having access to Roxy and Anna. I turned up to collect Anna from the childminders on my contact day, to find that the childminder wouldn't answer the door. I knew instantly what was going on and that the childminder had obviously been given strict instructions from Josie, to not hand Anna over to me. I went round to the back of the house, where I saw the childminder trying to hide from me. I hung around for a while and after about ten minutes Josie and the police turned up at the childminders. Initially, I was quite glad to see the police as I thought that things would get sorted once I explained the situation. But the police took Josie into the childminders house and after about five or ten minutes the police came out and informed me that I had to leave. When I explained the situation and showed them a copy of the court order, they simply dismissed what I had to say. Once again, this showed me the kind of bias that exists in our society towards mums over dads. And at that moment, I found myself on the receiving end of those prejudices as a father. As a father, it's heartbreaking to be in that situation. I felt utterly powerless against the injustice of what was happening to me. So, I decided I needed to take action to prevent Josie from breaching the order whenever she felt like it. I made an application to the family court to enforce the order that was in place. Enforcing an order, basically means that when an order is breached by either party, you have the right to apply for the order to be enforced. This then gives the court the power to issue a punishment for the breach which can be a fine, community service, or even a prison sentence. The hearing was scheduled within a few weeks of my application and it was in front of District Judge Jordan again, which I was pleased about. But it didn't go as I wanted it to. The judge simply asked us both if the contact was back to normal, which at this point it was. He decided not to enforce the order. I couldn't believe it! The message he had just sent out to Josie, was that the order was not worth the paper it was written on and that she was free to breach it as and when she pleased. I later came to discover that these child arrangement orders are seldom enforced, especially when a mother breaches the order. This sad fact renders most court orders useless.

God Speaks Again

I'd been a follower of Jesus for about two or three years by now, but I'd found that God spoke to me in so many ways. I'd never heard the audible voice of God, but he spoke to me through conversations I'd have with people, through messages I'd listen to at church, on GOD TV, or through my circumstances and even through challenges in my life. I'd been working at Royal Mail specialist services now for over a year and it was really starting to grind on me. The 3 am alarm wake-up calls were negatively affecting my mood and general well-being. I knew I had to get out. God started to show me that I had more inside me than simply doing a manual labour job. I think Mel could see it too and she really encouraged me to make more of my natural gifts and talents. Mel is such an encouraging person and she helped me to realise some of the potential I had. I loved listening to a pastor from our church called Paul Scanlon. I really connected with his practical messages and I vividly remember two messages he preached at church titled *'Destiny'* and *'Finding your God-Given Shape'*. I found them amazing! God spoke to me so powerfully through those messages. I remember hearing, *"What were you good at in school and what do you enjoy doing?"* All I ever loved at school was sport and I loved learning about the anatomy of the body when I did GCSE and then A-level PE. It also dawned on me that I'd learned so much from my time with Tommy over the years. He had healed me of so many different injuries and I'd gained so much knowledge from him. I knew I could use this knowledge to help other people. This led to me enrolling in a college course to become a qualified sports therapist. I went full throttle and I managed to gain four separate diplomas in several physical therapies. It took me just over a year. I did all this while working 50 hours a week at Royal Mail. But I'd always had a great work ethic and I knew all the time and hard work now was simply a means to an end. When I decided to enrol and gain my qualifications, I'd envisaged that I would work for a professional rugby club or football club in a Sports Therapist role. But after I became qualified, I explored my options and unfortunately, the opportunities were pretty much non-existent! However, with the support and belief from Mel, I decided to set up on my own as a Sports Therapist. It was an extremely challenging prospect, but one I was prepared for. I initially found a small treatment room to rent, set up a website, and began to offer some voucher deals. It meant I made almost no money from the treatments, but the purpose of it was to build up my client base as quickly as possible so that I could quit my job at Royal Mail. I said to Mel that once I was turning clients away because of my work commitments at Royal Mail, then this was the time to quit my job. After about three or four months, this started to happen, but I was still reluctant to leave my job at Royal Mail. I was fearful of not being able to earn enough money to pay my mortgage, bills, and to provide for my family. But typical of Mel, she gave me the push I needed and reminded me of what I'd said some months before. I will always be forever grateful to Mel for encouraging me to take that step of faith. In early 2012, I handed in my notice at Royal Mail and during those last two weeks at work, I felt like I was on cloud nine! I was irritating some of my work colleagues with how unusually happy I was at 4 am in the morning! I truly felt blessed at the prospect of fulfilling my God-given purpose. I knew it would be so rewarding to help others overcome their injuries. Being self-employed also gave me the freedom to control my own working hours which would allow me to spend more time with Mel and the kids, which was another huge blessing.

Old Friends

Around this time, I saw my old mate, Jamie Jones-Buchanan, being interviewed on a Sky Sports show called Super Leagues Supermen. I had lost contact with Jonesy since I retired from playing rugby. He was speaking to the interviewer, Brian Carney, about his life and career. Jonesy was enjoying a successful career at Leeds Rhinos and had already won multiple Grand Finals. He was a part of what would be known as The Golden Generation. Jonesy also spoke openly about his faith in Jesus Christ and how Jesus had changed his life. He talked about how he became born again, through a relationship with a Kiwi player at Leeds called Ali Lauiti'iti. It was amazing how we'd followed the same spiritual paths and listening to him talk inspired me to get back in contact with him. We lived less than a mile from each other. I phoned him and we arranged to meet up. It was like we'd never lost contact and it was so good to have such a great friend as a fellow believer. Jonesy is an encyclopaedia of knowledge when it comes to God's Word, so it was fantastic to talk to him about God and Jesus. It was clear we were both different people from when we were friends the first time around. He was passionate about his faith and he lived for his family and helping out in his community. He really was the type of person who would do anything for you.

Marriage

Marriage had not been something I had ever seriously considered. I had taken on the worldly attitude that marriage was just a 'bit of paper' and that it didn't make any difference to a relationship. But now that I was a Christian and in a committed relationship, my attitude towards marriage was beginning to change. In April 2012, I was invited to a men's Christian conference in North Yorkshire called Mighty Men. I went with a new Christian friend of mine called Mike. He was like me; he hadn't been brought up as a Christian but found his faith in his adulthood. We also shared the same passion for fishing too. At the conference, there was a speaker from South Africa called Angus Buchan. He was a well-known Christian evangelist. I had found out about him beforehand by watching a film about his life called Faith Like Potatoes. The movie made a big impact on me. It told his life story and about his conversion from being a miserable, beer-drinking, violent man, to becoming a powerful man of God. He went on to inspire a whole generation in South Africa. The movie even showed him raising someone from the dead through the power of Jesus' Name. He had a straightforward and practical style to his teaching and at the conference, Angus preached a powerful message about marriage and relationships. It really resonated with me and I felt convicted (the word 'convicted' simply means, 'to be convinced') by the Holy Spirit that me and Mel needed to get married. I realised that God created marriage and that I was living in sin by not being married. I discovered a Bible verse relating to marriage that says, *'Though one may be overpowered, two can defend themselves. A cord of three strands is not quickly broken'* Ecclesiastes 4:12. God is the third strand. I knew we needed to get married.

However, me being me and having the tendency to have to plan things out, I decided I was going to propose on my 30th birthday, which is on the 2 August, whilst we were on holiday in Lanzarote. It would be our first holiday abroad as a blended family. I wanted my proposal to be romantic and for the kids to be there too. But I was soon to discover that God had a sense of humour towards my plan. From the minute I decided to propose to Mel, almost everyone we knew started to ask us if we were going to get married. My face was a picture every time someone asked us the question. But I did my best to act as casually as possible and I don't think Mel ever suspected anything. I came up with a plan to take the engagement ring on holiday with me and propose on the night of my birthday. The time came and I was so nervous. I wanted it to be simply perfect. After our evening meal, I led us all down to the beachfront and took Roxy and Zac to one side, while Mel was standing with Anna in her buggy. I think Mel worked out that we were up to something. I asked Roxy and Zac to say to Mel, *"Will you do something for daddy?"* Then I got down on one knee and said, *"Will you marry me?"* Mel's reaction was priceless! I don't even remember her saying yes! She just took the ring and ran off squealing and jumping up and down, shouting to random people,

"I'm getting married!!" I will never forget the sight of her running and jumping for joy! When she eventually calmed down, we went to a bar and she bought the kids a mocktail each to celebrate. It was such a happy moment and I will forever have fond memories of that fantastic holiday! But such as life is, just when you feel that it's going to be smooth sailing, it throws you another right hook…..

I adore being at home with my family

Anna and me at Disneyworld, Florida, 2015

The day Mel and I were baptised at Life Church, Bradford

All of my family ready to attend a family wedding

Me and Zac on the Jane Tomlinson Fun Run

Our Wedding Day in 2013; one of the happiest days of my life!

Me with the great Tommy Smales just a few weeks before he went home to be with the Lord

Chapter 12
A Wedding And A Court Case

We decided that we wanted to get married as soon as possible. So, we arranged the date of the 16th February 2013, to get married at our home church, Life Church in Bradford. We also decided that we wanted to move to a new house after we got engaged. We needed more space as it was quite cramped with the five of us at home in our three bedroomed terraced house. Plus, we felt it would be a great way to start our marriage. But it was going to be almost impossible for us to get a new mortgage because both me and Mel had recently become self-employed. We were just earning enough to get by. And almost all mortgage providers wanted to see at least three years' accounts in order to approve a mortgage. But we decided to put our faith in God, and we prayed for God to make a way when it seemed like there was no way. I knew about a verse in Matthew 19:26, *'But Jesus looked at them and said to them, 'With men this is impossible, but with God all things are possible'"*.

A couple of weeks later I was having a conversation with a client of mine called Scott. He was a great guy and he was a successful businessman too. He'd been brought up in a rough council estate in Bradford and despite his business success, he was a very humble man. I was explaining to him about my frustration at not being able to get a new mortgage and move to a new house. He kindly offered me a few suggestions of how he thought it could be done and he gave me his friend's contact details, who was a mortgage broker. I spoke to Mel about it and we decided to contact Scott's friend. Our

talks were positive, and it was starting to look promising that we could get a mortgage approved, even though on paper, our credentials suggested otherwise. Miraculously, we managed to get a mortgage in principle and we also found the perfect house. It was a brand new four-bedroom detached property with a large garden and a garage in nearby Tong, Bradford. It would be amazing if we could manage to buy this house! It had been the show home on a plot of new houses, but it was one of the last houses left. It was also fully kitted out with lots of furniture and beds, etc, just as it was with a show home. However, we needed to sell our house first and we realised that could take a while. Me and Mel quickly got to work on our house. We spruced it up with a lick of paint and we managed to get it looking immaculate. We put the house on the market, and I was so confident it would sell that I said to Mel, *"I think the first person that views our house will buy it"*. But sadly, we had very little interest from anyone. Nobody came to view the house for the first seven weeks. Then a local man came to view it and he put in an offer straight away. Wow! We negotiated on the asking price and fortunately, he bought it. I had been proven right, the first person that viewed the house, bought it! God had come through when it looked impossible. Even better, the man was buying it as an investment to rent out, therefore he wasn't in a chain that could hold things up. So, we made an offer on the house in Tong straight away and we managed to get a great deal, as it had been up for sale for so long. We were over the moon to secure our dream home! We were so thankful! I really believe that God sent Scott to help us in this season in our lives. He even provided us with his HGV to help us out on the day we moved! We will be forever grateful to Scott for what he did for us and how he helped us to get our dream home. What confirmed to me that Scott was sent by God, was that just as quickly as he appeared in my life, he disappeared. Go figure?

Our wedding day came around and it was more than we could have imagined. With Life Church being such a modern, vibrant church, it was great for some of our friends and family to experience it. I think it was an eye-opener for many. Mind you, we did have to arrange the day strategically, so that it fell on a weekend when we had Roxy and Anna. We knew that Josie would have never agreed to let Roxy and Anna be a part of our big day. But it worked out perfectly and Roxy and Anna were both bridesmaids at our wedding. Roxy was super excited and, in the lead up to the wedding, Mel took the girls to choose their bridesmaid dresses. We hired Roxy her own sweet stall from eBay for the wedding reception. She loved serving sweets to the guests and we even managed to get her a personalised apron made with 'Roxy's Sweet Shop' embroidered on it. But I really cannot take credit for any of that as Mel was in charge of anything creative for the wedding. She even had me, and the kids, go into the local woods to get tree branches that she and the kids painted and created into pretty décor for the wedding reception. They were so good that the venue decided to keep the tree decorations up permanently. Mel, of course, looked stunning in her wedding dress. Zac was five years old and was given the role of ring bearer which he fully embraced. My best man, Karl, who I had been mates with since school, did a great job of embarrassing me in his speech. He also managed to make the wedding party feel uneasy with some of his explicit stories of nights out from when we were younger. It was such a memorable day and it certainly wasn't your standard wedding.

CSA

This was certainly a season of my life that brought me many trials and testing moments. Shortly after we got married, I was shocked to receive a court summons from the Child Support Agency (CSA), claiming that I owed them over five thousand pounds in child maintenance for Roxy and Anna. I knew this couldn't be correct, as I had always paid what they said I had to. In fact, after I paid Josie three thousand pounds to set up in her new home, we agreed on a monthly figure that I would pay her as maintenance for Roxy and Anna. The day after I paid her the first monthly payment, I was shocked to receive a phone call from the CSA. They informed me that they were ringing on behalf of Josie to collect child maintenance payments. At first, I was confused, so I explained to them that I had paid her our agreed monthly payment, just the day before and that I had proof of this payment. I explained that I had also paid Josie three thousand pounds just a month prior. The CSA representative explained to me that anything that I had paid to Josie before this phone call could not be considered. Wow! I could not believe their policies and that they could be so apathetic towards the facts of the matter. But I was soon to learn that the many horror stories I'd heard about the CSA were true. I experienced first-hand that as a father, the CSA labels you as a 'scumbag' father who wants to avoid the responsibility of providing for his children. Their system is dire, and I would sometimes receive three letters from them on the same day, all stating different things. Josie clearly knew how the system worked and deliberately devised a plan to detract more money from me. She was being deliberately deceptive for her own financial gain. Some may have thought that she had played a blinder and that she was working the system to her benefit. I simply could not afford to pay what they were asking for. I stuck to my principles and I refused to pay her the five thousand pounds they claimed I owed. But I learned that the CSA have various powers of authority. I just couldn't believe the injustice of it all! I still, to this day, do not know how they got the figure of over five thousand pounds that I owed! They had been taking money directly from my wages for over a year, so how did they get it so wrong? I was willing to go to court and defend myself because I knew I didn't owe them a penny. The months building up to the court hearing were incredibly stressful. Fortunately, I've always been a mentally strong individual but the thought of the CSA slapping a liability order on me was so unjust and it made me sick to my stomach. I also learned that this type of injustice was happening to so many other dads. Some fathers get hit with figures of over £100,000 that the CSA claim they unfairly owe. They can financially ruin men and some mothers use this as a weapon to get revenge on their ex-partner. I learned that the statistics of men taking their own lives due to the CSA pursuing them for money they didn't owe were through the roof!

The court hearing came around and I went along, took all my paperwork, including bank statements, wage slips, etc. I pleaded my case and showed them all my paperwork which proved what I had paid every month. But sadly, it came to no avail. The court wasn't interested in anything I presented to them and took no notice of what I had to say. They issued me with a liability order for over five thousand pounds. This meant that if I didn't pay the debt, then they had several powers to obtain the money from me, such as putting an order of sale on our family home to force me to sell it to pay the debt. They could also put me in prison or recommend I fulfil community service. These may sound like extreme measures, but it happens to innocent dads every day and people don't even realise it. The thought of losing our newly bought dream home really put a lot of stress on me mentally and physically. I thought I was handling it by trying to burden the responsibility myself. But after a while, Mel pointed out to me that she could see the effect it was having on me. I was becoming snappy and short-tempered with her and the kids, which is not like me. I was at a dead-end and I just didn't know which way to turn.

I decided to turn to God.

I'd heard of a scripture in Peter 5:7 that said, *"Give all your worries and cares to God, for he cares about you."* So, I decided to do just that. But I didn't know what that looked like and how to do it. I prayed and I surrendered the whole situation to Jesus. Within days, I began to feel more at peace with the situation. Then, within a week, one of my clients at work explained to me that he'd had some similar issues with the CSA in the past. He told me about a company based in the Midlands called NACSA. They were legal experts on the laws surrounding the CSA circumstances and they helped people get to the bottom of their CSA case. I gave them a call and they indicated that they could help me. They assigned me a caseworker and I had to pay them a monthly fee while they worked on my case. But I felt it was worth it if they were able to get me justice. It also helped ease a lot of the pressure on me because NACSA dealt with any letters or phone calls that I would have previously received from the CSA. Over about six months they managed to get to the bottom of my case and by October 2013 they came back to me with some news about my case. And it was great news! They informed me that the CSA owed *me* money! Wow, unbelievable, eh?! So, the CSA had taken me to court, and they were satisfied that I was liable to pay over five thousand pounds in unpaid child maintenance. But in fact, they owed *me* money. That just shows you how corrupt the CSA can be. In my opinion, it's criminal and it's happening every single day to many good, honest, law-abiding fathers, some of whom just can't take the pressure and injustice of it all. It is heartbreaking and it has to stop!

Resisting God's Calling

I was now settled in my job as a Sports Therapist. I loved it and helping people for a living was a huge blessing. But God was about to call me to step out in obedience for Him. However, I wasn't at all ready or sure about what God had in mind. I'd been free from porn addiction for about three years now and God had helped me to grasp a real understanding of how and why porn addiction had dominated me for so long. God started to speak to my heart about sharing my story with other people, especially young people, about the harmful effects of pornography and the dangers. The problem is much worse now with young kids having access to an unlimited amount of pornography on their smartphones and other devices. There isn't anywhere on the national schools' curriculum to educate young people about it. For over six months, God would not leave me alone about stepping out to share my story with others. It felt like almost every message I heard at church, on Christian radio, on GOD TV, or in our Life house group, was as if God was calling me to just do it. I realised that with God, he rarely gives you the specific details of what the calling will look like which can be very annoying! But still, I resisted God's calling. The very thought of sharing with other people how I was addicted to porn and sex just made me squirm with shame and embarrassment. Internally, I argued with God about it for over six months. I even told God to find someone else to do it and that he must have got the wrong person!

But I began to realise that God doesn't make mistakes when it comes to choosing people to carry out His work. I discovered something in the Bible that the apostle Paul said that helped me to understand how God uses people. In 2 Corinthians 12:9, Paul wrote,

'Each time he said, "My grace is all you need. My power works best in weakness." So now I am glad to boast about my weaknesses, so that the power of Christ can work through me. That's why I take pleasure in my weaknesses, and in the insults, hardships, persecutions, and troubles that I suffer for Christ. And so, the weaker I get, the stronger I become"'

I eventually surrendered to God's will and I 'stepped out of the boat', just as Peter did when Jesus called him to walk on water. But I must admit, it was terrifying! I wasn't sure where to start. However, I remembered that my good friend Mike and his wife Sophie ran a youth group from their local church in Harrogate. I spoke to Mike about what God had called me to do. He was really encouraging, and he invited me to speak to their youth group. I went along and I was so nervous! I made some notes about what I was going to speak about. But it's fair to say, I was ordinary at best! When I started to speak, my legs started to uncontrollably shake. I felt like I was dying. It didn't feel like it was going very well. But the teenagers seemed quite engaged and asked questions at the end of my talk. Mike told me about a charity called The Naked Truth Project based in Manchester. They had a ministry that specifically helped people with porn addiction and educated young people on the harmful effects. So, I decided to contact their main man, a guy called Ian Henderson. Ian was super supportive, and he invited me to go along with him to a high school in Blackburn, where he was presenting a lesson on 'The Harmful Effects of Pornography'. It was a great learning experience for me, and I picked up so much knowledge and wisdom from the day I spent with Ian. It really gave me the confidence I needed, and it inspired me to share my story with many more young people. And I did just that. I set up a website called Porn on the Brain and I contacted schools, offering my services. I also knew another guy through church who was a former alcoholic who overcame his addiction. His name is Tom and he shared his story in schools and with businesses. Tom invited me along to watch him deliver his message at a school in Leeds. He was an inspirational speaker and I was close to tears listening to his life story. Tom mentored me and gave me lots of tips to hone my public speaking skills. I will be forever grateful to everyone who helped me on this journey. I began to get more speaking opportunities in schools and a few church youth groups. I got some fantastic feedback which was so encouraging. My public speaking skills were certainly improving with all the practice I was getting. It was an amazing feeling knowing I was making a massive difference in the lives of many young people. I wished someone had visited my school to teach me about the harmful effects of pornography. I know it would have opened my eyes to the negative effects that porn was having on me. I was also getting opportunities to go on TV programmes. Then, through a good friend of mine called Warren, who is the CEO of Sports Chaplaincy UK, I got asked to do an interview on Revelation TV to speak about my life. Off the back of this interview, I got contacted by The Salvation Army and a Christian charity called Ten: Ten who both made videos about my story to help teach young people about the dangers of porn. I also joined up with The Naked Truth Project who deliver some amazing work in schools and the wider community. Sadly, we still live in a world that consistently fails to recognise the damage that pornography does to people and our society. It's like a drug and it's wrecking the lives of people and their relationships every day. Fortunately, I am blessed to continue to do God's work in this area to this very day.

Chapter 13

New Arrival

Four months after we got married, me and Mel went on an eleven-night Mediterranean cruise for our honeymoon. We had an amazing time and made the most of our time away without the kids. Maybe we had too much of a good time, because 10 months later, on the 19th April 2014, our beautiful new baby daughter was born, and she became the newest addition to the Kirk family. We were all over the moon! Roxy, Zac, and Anna loved having a baby sister and Harlow just added to our wonderful family unit. Mel went through the mill during a 17-hour labour which ended with her having a Caesarean. However, Mel being Mel, she still maintained her appetite and mid-way through her labour, she sent me out to get her a takeaway pizza. Mel pushed through the pain barrier and I was super proud of her! I was in the operating theatre when the doctors performed the Caesarean and I did my best to encourage and support Mel. I held Mel's hand and watched as the doctor sliced her open, which was pretty brutal. It was like watching an animal being slaughtered. I'm not the type to be squeamish, but that was difficult to watch. But it was so lovely to be involved in Harlow's birth as I had missed out on all that with Anna. It felt very similar to when Roxy and Anna were born. I felt such an overwhelming feeling of love when I first held Harlow. She was so beautiful and perfect!

Settled

The following years proved to be quite a settled time for us as a family. I changed my work schedule to just three days per week instead of six so that I could be with Harlow and collect the other three children from school. This also allowed Mel to get straight back into work. She was now a self-employed hair extension tutor and within a month of Harlow being born, Mel was working again. Mel has never been the type to be content pottering around the house, so it was great for her to get back into the swing of things. We juggled the childcare between us both. For the first six months, Mel would express breast milk for me to give Harlow on the days that I was at home with her. It was so comical, seeing Mel with the breast pump attached to her in the evening, like a cow being milked. We laughed about it, and it was all good banter! I know she was glad when she no longer had to express breast milk anymore though, as it was getting painful for her.

I just loved spending quality time with my amazing family. During the week, I would collect the kids from school, and I would regularly take them to the park, swimming, or to a play gym where we had made some great memories. As a dad, I was always conscious of not making the same mistakes my dad did with me. I wanted them to feel free and comfortable to talk to me if they felt low or were struggling emotionally. I also felt it was important to show them lots of physical affection, so I always hugged and kissed them and told them how much I loved them, at every opportunity I got. This was something that I lacked from my father and it affected me negatively as I was growing up and into my adulthood. God showed me very clearly, the reason I had found it difficult to make close male friendships and bonds was because of my relationship with my dad. I just didn't trust men with my emotions, therefore, I never allowed myself to fully open up or be vulnerable with other men. I'd built my walls high. But God also helped me to heal from this. I now have several close male friends, praise God! I really wanted the best start in life for my children and although I knew that I would never be the perfect father, I just wanted to be all I could be for them. In fact, one of the most powerful prayers I have ever prayed is, *"Lord, show me how to be a better husband and a better father"*. Because we didn't have Roxy and Anna full time, it spurred me to make the most of every moment I had with them.

One positive family trait that I wanted to continue from my own childhood were family holidays. We went on some fantastic holidays in this country and abroad. One holiday that wasn't so memorable for Mel, was a camping trip we went on when Harlow was just four months old. I borrowed a tent from my mate Jonesy and some other camping essentials from another mate of mine. We went to a quiet camping site in Harrogate for two nights. It had a fishing lake on it, so I took some of my fishing tackle and I was able to take the kids on their first fishing adventure. I loved fishing as a kid, and I wanted them to experience it too. Me and the kids loved it, but Mel wasn't so keen. Unfortunately, the typical British summer weather struck, and it ended up being a cold and wet few days. Mel hated the whole experience and she begged me and the kids to stay in a hotel for the second night, to which I declined, letting her know that if we're camping, then we were all in and there was no bailing out. She wasn't happy, but to her credit, she braved the elements and put on a brave smile for me and the kids. Over the years we were fortunate enough to experience some warmer, more exotic destinations. In the summer of 2015, we went to Disney World in Florida for two weeks. We'd always dreamed of taking the kids there. We were all super excited! We had a villa with a pool, and we hired a car for two weeks. We had theme park and water park passes for the whole two weeks and we made the most of it. We arrived at our villa late at night and by this time we were all absolutely exhausted from the long trip. We woke up on the first morning of our dream holiday, and we all wanted to check out the pool. But to our horror, we were faced with a snake occupying our pool! Mel and the kids weren't impressed, so I did my best impression of the late Steve Irwin and removed the snake with some BBQ tongs. Later in the holiday, Zac's drawstring fell out of his swimming shorts while he was in the pool and it laid still at the bottom of the pool. It looked like a snake. Roxy was having a nap in her bedroom when this happened, so when she woke up and came out, I decided to play a trick on her. I pretended the drawstring was a snake and told her I would catch it and get it out of the pool. I once again did my best impression of Steve Irwin, which ended up looking more like Crocodile Dundee. Roxy's face was a picture. But she soon realised it wasn't a snake and that dad was playing a mean trick on her. We also discovered that the area of America where we were, didn't seem very tolerant of interracial families. I'd always thought that America was ahead of Britain regarding racism, given their history, but it appeared not. Don't get me wrong, I'm not saying that we felt unwelcome in any way, but there was a sense that some people found it difficult to comprehend that we were a family. One example was when Mel took Roxy on a theme park ride and the park attendant didn't believe that Roxy was with Mel.

It was my birthday while we were there, so Mel and the kids were keen to surprise me with a big chocolate cake. They took it upon themselves to roll around Walmart like some Royal Marine cadets. Their plan included sending me into Walmart to grab a few bits, while I thought they were waiting patiently in the car. But unbeknown to me, they sneaked in after me, desperately trying to avoid me. They had to get in and out before I got back to the car, so they didn't blow their cover. They succeeded and I didn't suspect a thing. Later that evening we celebrated my birthday at a really nice restaurant. I was pleasantly surprised when the waitress brought out a massive chocolate cake after the meal. Mel and the kids sang Happy Birthday to me with massive grins on their faces. It was then that they revealed the lengths they had gone to in order to surprise me. I know the kids found it all great fun and I so appreciated the efforts they had gone to. It can't have been easy, trying to sneak around a supermarket with an eight, seven, four, and a one-year-old. They all made it such a memorable birthday and holiday! We only need to mention 'Bob Evans' and we all think of the restaurant where we would regularly go for a hearty All American breakfast!

During another summer holiday, we went to Turkey where the heat was unbearable at times. It was over 40 degrees almost every day. Then another year we went to Majorca. It took me a while, but I began to embrace the fact that our holidays were never going to be relaxing for me and Mel having four young children, yet I just loved messing around in the pool or the sea with the kids. In Turkey, while on the beach, I spent about two hours with Roxy and Zac, trying to catch fish under the water with our bare hands. I knew it was impossible and that we would never catch a fish in this way, but I just loved playing and building those positive memories as a family. Then in Majorca, one day, me, Roxy, Zac, and Anna swam out in the sea quite far on the lilo. Roxy panicked and yelled that she saw a jellyfish, but we weren't sure if she was mistaken or not. Then about ten seconds later, Anna screamed that she had been stung. I pulled us towards the rocks and got all the kids out of the water. Anna had been stung and she was upset. Fortunately, when we got back to the beach and calmed her down, she was fine. It was also a great adventure story for her to tell her friends when she got back to school. But sadly, events would soon materialise, meaning this would be our last ever family holiday together with all six of us.

Christmas 2017 was certainly one to remember. Mel and the kids had been wanting a pet dog for years and I'd always resisted. I wasn't keen on having the responsibility of looking after a dog. Both me and Mel were out of the house most days between Monday to Friday. But I finally gave in and I agreed to get a dog, which we decided to give to the kids as their main present on Christmas Day. We did our research and decided on a Bichon Frise. They were small, cute, fun, and a friendly breed of dog. It was a female puppy and we managed to get her on the 23 December. We decided to name her Skyla. Mel's mum kindly offered to have her overnight, to allow us to surprise the kids on Christmas morning. I was super excited for the kids, but I was also excited myself. I was desperate for a dog when I was a kid. I begged my parents to let me have one for years, but they wouldn't get me one. I really didn't want to be like my dad with my kids. Being an introvert and not very social, if I'd had a pet dog, it would have been like my best mate and I would have taken it everywhere with me. Christmas morning came around and I'd sneaked out of the house the night before to collect Skyla. Then, after the kids had all opened their presents, we announced that we had one special present left to give them. I will never forget their reaction when we brought Skyla into the living room. We got them all to turn facing the wall, then told them to turn around once Mel walked in holding Skyla. Their faces were a picture. Their reaction was totally priceless! They fell over each other trying to get to Skyla and they were overjoyed. So, Kirk family member number seven was here, and we were all so happy!

In 2018, when Harlow started primary school and Roxy moved up to high school, the school run took on legendary status. All four kids were now at different schools. I would set off from home in Bradford to pick Roxy up from her school in Leeds, then drive just around the corner to Anna's school to collect her. Then we would drive across Leeds to pick up Zac and finally to Bradford to collect Harlow from her school. We also had to put Harlow into an after-school club for an hour. It was a twenty-mile plus round trip which took me about ninety minutes to complete. But I had no complaints about doing it. I cherished the two days I picked them up from school as it was such a blessing to have all my kids together and it was amazing to see them grow so close over the years. I am so proud of every single one of them. They are all super talented and have their own unique personalities. Each one was excelling in school too. In fact, I could fill most of this book with how fantastic they are! Roxy has always been a super talented writer from being incredibly young and she is so creative. I also took her to gymnastics and trampolining club, which she excelled at and she started playing rugby at 11 years old. Zac has always had a superb talent for sport and loves playing football. By the time he was eleven years old, he'd had interest from some professional clubs, including Manchester City and Sheffield United Academies, and briefly played at Barnsley Academy. Anna is such a loving, kind girl, with a great sense of humour. She loved doing kickboxing classes with Zac on a weekend. And then there's Harlow. She has such a strong, fiery character, but so loving and gentle too.

I burst with love for them all and that will never change!

Chapter 14

Parental Alienation

On Good Friday, 2018, we were due to pick up Roxy and Anna at 9 am for the Easter weekend as per the court order. Mel offered to do me a favour and collect the girls from the police station. I had just dropped the girls off the previous evening at 8 pm which is about an eighteen-mile round trip to and from our house, so I was glad when Mel offered to collect them. I know you might be thinking that it's ridiculous that we would have to do this and that it makes more sense for them to simply stay on Thursday night, but Josie would never allow this to happen. I had asked her numerous times over the years, whenever the days fell, which meant I was dropping them at 8 pm on a Thursday, then collecting them again, just 13 hours later. But she'd always said, "*No*", and gave what I felt was some lame reason as to why.

When Mel arrived at the police station car park, Josie was already sitting in her car waiting. When she saw Mel driving in, she immediately set off to drive away in her car with the girls. Josie was ranting and raving in her car and gesturing at Mel. She was clearly enraged that Mel had come to collect the girls. Mel rang me to tell me what had just happened. I just couldn't believe that Josie could be so petty, eight years on after we'd separated. I knew it would have a negative impact on the girls having to witness their mum's behaviour and would have been traumatic for them. I messaged Josie, to tell her to bring the girls back. She said she would only hand the girls over to me. So, in the end, I had to go down myself, along with Mel, Zac, and Harlow, to collect them from the police station. When I collected them, Anna was upset. I wasn't surprised, having to witness her mum enraged, ranting and shouting! But Josie had no concept of the harm that her actions were causing the girls. I had already noticed over the past year or so that Anna had some mild anxiety and I strongly suspected it could have been caused by Josie's unrestrained and negative view of me and Mel. Knowing Josie as I did, she wouldn't be shy about verbalising her hatred of me and Mel in the presence of the girls. I'd never communicated my concern up to now, as I knew that anything I said to Josie would fall on deaf ears. She wasn't the type of person who could take any constructive criticism on board or take steps to improve herself. Even more so if the criticism came from me. But as I noticed things develop, for my own conscience, I had to say something. I was convinced that she wouldn't take any notice, but at least I could live contentedly, knowing that I'd highlighted her behaviour and how it was negatively impacting the girls. I even sent her a link to a few psychological articles that I felt were relevant. One was a psychology article about Emotional Incest. I'd initially heard about this from a marriage teaching that I regularly watched. This teaching focused on blended families and I learned that this psychological behaviour is common in parents who have separated. What happens is that one parent will emotionally 'lean' or 'prop themselves up' on their child. I'd witnessed Josie do this from the moment we split up and it concerned me that this behaviour would do some harm to Roxy and Anna. But I also had to take some responsibility for Josie's behaviour. I was the one who cheated on her, more times than I could remember, and I'd hurt her so much by leaving when she was six months pregnant. Sadly, my message to Josie made no difference. In fact, she used the messages to attempt to tarnish the girl's view of me. Later, Roxy told me that she had seen some text messages I had sent to her mum and that her mum was upset. Also, about a year before this incident, when Roxy was ten years old and Anna was seven years old, they told Mel that their mum had revealed to them that I had cheated on her. Although this was, of course, true, I was convinced that Josie's agenda was to paint me out as the villain and make the girls feel sorry for her. I also learned that all this is part of a psychological process called 'parental alienation'. I began to study about it in-depth after I watched a Ted Talk by Dr Jennifer Harman, who is a professor of Psychology at Colorado State University. In recent years, it has become a recognised form of domestic violence and child abuse. What happens is that a child is subject to the negative views and opinions of one parent towards another, resulting in the psychological manipulation of the child, by poisoning them against the other parent. I'd always suspected that over the years, Josie had drip-fed her negative views and attitude about us to the girls. But because we had the girls almost half the time and had formed such a close, loving family bond, I believe it weakened some of the negativity that Josie tried to spread with her rumours about us. I even spoke with an active magistrates' judge from the south of England who was a Christian. He told me how he sees parental alienation almost every day in the family court. He explained to me how common it was and how he mainly saw mothers who were guilty of it. He shared the same frustrations as me and told me how he'd not seen his daughters for over twenty years. So sad.

Over the years since becoming a Born Again Christian, I'd learned to forgive the many people who'd hurt me, including Josie and some of my own family. Jesus famously said about the people who were crucifying Him on the Cross, *"Father, forgive them, for they don't know what they are doing"*, Luke 23:34.

I understood that much of Josie's behaviour since we'd split came from a place of hurt and that she didn't really know what she was doing. She was acting out of that fleshly desire for revenge. I'd also learned a valuable lesson that forgiving sets you free. Holding onto unforgiveness is like drinking poison and expecting the other person to die. It doesn't work and it only breeds bitterness and resentment.

Also, I was acutely aware that me and Mel parented very differently from Josie. My perception historically was that Josie had some insecurities and was an emotionally needy individual, so she was desperate to be the favoured parent. Therefore, she parented in an unhealthy way. I was starting to realise that she allowed the girls to do whatever they wanted and put in place little or no boundaries, rules, or discipline. It concerned me greatly and I knew this wasn't good for any child. Plus, I realised that because of this and the parental alienation, as the girls got older, they may choose to spend most of their time with their mum. It would have been easy for us to lower our standards of parenting so that the girls favoured us, but we knew we had to stick to our own convictions of the right way to parent and do what was best for them.

School Drama

In September 2018, Anna started Year 3 in primary school and had just turned 8 years old. I emailed the headteacher, Mr Bamgill, to let him know that due to my circumstances, Mel may be collecting Anna on the odd occasion when I couldn't get there. He replied to let me know it was fine and that he had passed on the relevant information to Anna's teacher. That same day, Mel came with me to pick the kids up from school. She went in to collect Anna and was chatting with Anna's teacher in the school reception area. Just as she was about to leave with Anna, the school Child Protection Officer, Mrs James, pounced on Anna and pulled her away from Mel and locked Anna in the back office. Mrs James was yelling *"Safeguarding issues!!"* towards Mel and other members of staff. Mel was totally stunned! I was sitting outside in the car with Roxy, totally unaware of what was going on. Then Mel rang me from inside the school to tell me what was happening. I was furious and I knew full well why this was happening. Josie's cousin worked at the school as a receptionist and she'd always been Josie's eyes and ears in the school. I'd had other issues over the years that I'd anticipated from the outset. For example, I would not receive information about Roxy and Anna's school performances and sports days, etc. It was usually anything to do with parents' attendance to an event. I knew it was Josie and her cousin trying to block any correspondence getting to me. It's so sad and selfish I know, but the last thing Josie wanted to see was me and Mel at the girl's school performances. I had multiple meetings with the headteacher over the years about it and it did seem to make some difference initially, but soon after, the same thing would happen. This was just another example of Josie's need for control. She couldn't bear the thought of Mel collecting Anna from school, so she did whatever she could to make sure that didn't happen. Anyway, with my blood boiling, I walked into the school reception and proceeded to tell Josie's cousin and Mrs James exactly what I thought of them. The headteacher, Mr Bamgill, threatened to kick me out of the school if I didn't calm down. But I was well justified in my frustrations, considering what had just happened. It was utterly disgraceful, but I managed to keep a level of composure. Mrs James was supposed to be the Child Protection Officer, but she'd just assaulted my 8-year-old daughter who was now sitting by herself, in the school office, sobbing! Mel even went into the office to comfort Anna, but she was physically pushed out by another member of staff. Unbelievable! Eventually, they handed Anna over to me and Mel, but I was livid about the whole situation. I knew that the school certainly would not have treated a mother in this manner. It was just another example of the prejudice that exists in our society against fathers. Over the ensuing days, I was in communication with the headteacher. Mr Bamgill had always struck me as being a weak leader and he told me that he needed to get advice from Leeds City Council's legal team, on what to do about Mel picking Anna up. I was astonished that he even needed to do this. Where was the common sense? Mel had been Anna's step mum from the day she was born and if he needed any legal confirmation then he had it in the court order, which stated, *'upon the court considering the CAFCASS report dated 4th April 2011 and noting there are no safeguarding concerns in relation to Melanie Kirk'*. It was there in black and white! Furthermore, the school had had a copy of the court order since Roxy started at the school, some seven years prior.

Thankfully, common sense prevailed (or so I thought), and the school contacted me to say that they'd had confirmation from Leeds City Council that Mel could pick Anna up from school. I just needed to make sure that Anna's teacher was aware of this on the day. At the same time, I arranged a meeting with Mr Bamgill to iron out any issues that might arise when Mel comes to collect Anna. You see, I knew that Josie would be seething with the school's decision and I anticipated that Josie would use her cousin to inform her of when Mel came to collect Anna. When me and Mel arrived at the meeting with Mr Bamgill and Mrs James, we were shocked to hear that the school had made an about-turn on their decision and that Mel could not pick Anna up. How could this be!? They went on to tell me that Josie had sent a letter that had resulted in Leeds City Council changing their decision. When I asked to see this letter, Mr Bamgill refused to show it to me. This felt so sly to me. I just couldn't believe what was happening. It was unlawful for the school to do this. I was flabbergasted, as well as furious! However, I'd come to realise that we lived in a society where mum's rights trumped fathers' rights every time. In situations like this, mum generally got what mum wanted. So, me and Mel got to work on writing letters of complaints about the incident, to the school, the board of governors and the department of education. The fact of the matter was, Anna had been assaulted by Mrs James, which was a criminal offence! They had overstepped the mark in the way they had treated Anna and Mel. However, as we progressed through the complaint's procedure, we soon learned that all schools are self-governed and were accountable to no one. All the staff involved, covered for each other and no action was taken. What a joke!

Instagram

I was aware that Josie had allowed Roxy to have a mobile phone from the age of ten years old. Personally, I wouldn't have allowed any of my kids to have a phone at this age, as I felt it was too young.

But Josie allowed her to have one and I wasn't one for interfering with her parenting decisions, so I kept my mouth shut.

In December 2018, when Roxy was eleven years old, Mel discovered that Roxy had an Instagram account. The discovery of her Instagram account wasn't too shocking to me, as I expected that she'd have various social media accounts. But I was horrified to see that Roxy was made up to look like an eighteen-year-old on her profile picture. Roxy was dressed in a short skirt, belly top, makeup, fake tan and false eyelashes at eleven years old! As any loving father would, I wanted to protect her. What was worse was that I knew that Josie had most likely taken the profile picture and encouraged her to dress like this for the picture. Furthermore, Instagram's own rules state that you must be thirteen years old to have an Instagram account. So, I decided to speak to Roxy about it the next time she was staying with us. I had a feeling that Roxy would deny having an Instagram account, so I decided to record our conversation on my phone. I felt I might need this down the line at some point. After our dinner one evening, I sat down with Roxy one to one and asked her the question about whether she had any social media on her phone. I was conscious that I had to approach the subject in a calm, mild manner in order to put her at ease that she wasn't in trouble. As I thought she would, she said she didn't. I then showed Roxy her own Instagram account on my phone. She told me it was an old account that she no longer accessed. When I pointed out to her that the picture was in her newly decorated bedroom at her mum's, she still claimed it was an old account. I knew she was lying to me, which is always hard to hear as a parent, but I remained calm and collected and I tried to reassure her that she wasn't in any trouble. How could she be? Her mum had allowed her to have the account. Roxy then began to get very upset. I gently explained to Roxy the dangers of displaying herself in this way on social media. I explained that there are many men out there, who are looking to take advantage of young girls and that her picture was exactly the type of profile they would be looking for. I also explained that it was illegal for anyone under the age of thirteen to have an Instagram account. I then gave her the opportunity to delete the account within the next few days or I would report it to Instagram, who would take it down as she was underage. I knew this would make me unpopular with Roxy, but I was doing what I thought was the right and proper thing to do as a father to protect my daughter. I also messaged Josie and asked her if she knew that Roxy had the account and she replied to me, saying yes, she did know that Roxy had an Instagram account. A couple of days later, I checked to see if Roxy had deleted her account, only to find that her username and profile picture had been changed. I realised my efforts to protect her had been fruitless. However, worse was to come and the corruption I was about to experience in the family court system was going to be off the scale……

Chapter 15

Back In Court

At the beginning of 2019, we made the difficult decision to make a new court application for a shared residence order. The idea of this was to hopefully amend the current contact order that had been in place since 2011, and for it to be replaced with a new shared residence order. We felt that the current order needed updating. We wanted it to include Mel being able to collect Anna from school and to increase our holiday time with the girls from one week abroad to two consecutive weeks. Roxy and Anna had missed out on a two-week Mediterranean cruise we went on as a family, in September 2017, simply because Josie wouldn't let them come. We also wanted to be able to drop the girls back home a few hours later than we already did on Sundays, as we would sometimes have to cut short any days out in order to drop the girls back at 5 pm. You'd hope these arrangements would be easy to sort out with your ex-partner, especially after being separated for nearly nine years. But sadly, that wasn't the case with Josie. I felt that she had an unhealthy need to control the time I spent with the girls. And, you may be wondering, does she have a partner? Yes, she has been in a relationship for over eight years to date. However, I'm not convinced of the quality of their relationship as they have never lived together. I suspect the reason for this is because government benefits would have to end if she declared that she lived with someone.

Mel also applied for Parental Responsibility (PR) for Roxy and Anna at the same time. The two applications would be rolled into one, so it wouldn't cost us any extra for this application. Our purpose of this application was mainly to protect Zac and Harlow's relationship with Roxy and Anna as we were certain that if anything happened to me, then Josie would definitely not allow the girls to continue to see Zac and Harlow. This was a horrible thought as the kids had such a close bond. We also felt that if Mel had PR, then she wouldn't have any problems collecting Anna from school as she would have the same rights as a biological parent. Before we made the court application, we spoke to the girls about their feelings about it. We explained things as best we could, and they seemed happy with what we were trying to achieve. Roxy did have a concern that she didn't want to sleepover during the week, because she still wanted to walk to school with her friends. I respected her wishes on this and I was happy for her to still do this. We knew that CAFCASS would speak to the girls about their thoughts and feelings and I hoped they would feel free to say how they felt. But I did have concerns that they would feel under pressure from their mum. When Josie received the court papers, she then made her own application to the court, which was an application to vary the current court order. She was stating that the girls now wanted to spend less time with us. It was blatantly obvious that this was her retaliating to our application. She'd never mentioned that the girls wanted to spend less time with us up to now. It was obvious what she was doing but I was confident that anyone, including a CAFCASS officer and the court, would be able to see through what she was trying to do.

Thus, the first court hearing was scheduled for February 2019. Nothing much happened at this hearing. A CAFCASS officer had done a telephone interview with me, Mel, and Josie. There wasn't much to report, however, I did highlight to the CAFCASS officer, that I had concerns about Josie psychologically manipulating Roxy and Anna. It also came to light that Josie was on medication for anxiety. The report read, *"Ms Smith advised she has suffered anxiety since 2009 and takes medication which is overseen by her GP"*. I'd known she suffered from anxiety and panic attacks when we were together. At this hearing, the court ordered CAFCASS to do what they call a Section 7 report, which is normal, and I expected this to happen. One of the purposes of this is to ascertain the wishes and feelings of the children. But they also speak to both parents including Mel. One thing that did concern me, was that Josie would now get busy working on the girls to manipulate them in such a way, to get them to say what she wanted them to say to CAFCASS. But I hoped that wouldn't be the case. The next court date was set for the end of May, which by then, the CAFCASS Section 7 report would have been completed.

Family life went along as normal, which was fantastic as always. We'd even booked a ten-night summer holiday to Ibiza for us all which we were so looking forward to. We'd never been to Ibiza and we were so excited. The CAFCASS report was due to be completed on the 13 May and we were due in court the following week for the next hearing. I'd noticed that Roxy wasn't quite herself. I couldn't put my finger on it, but I put it down to her getting a bit older and starting to go through puberty. The CAFCASS officer was a woman called Deena. Me and Mel were invited to meet her at her office, where we discussed with her our family and our reasons for making the new court application. She called me a few weeks later once she'd spoken with Roxy and Anna. She told me that during her time with Anna, she had asked her if she wanted to write a letter to the judge. Anna did and she wrote, *"Dear Judge, I would like you to know that I am happy with the amount of time I spend with my Dad. I don't want it to change. I like seeing Zac and Harlow"*. It was what I'd expected Anna to say. However, Deena also informed me the things that Roxy had said to her while speaking to her. Initially, I was shocked at some of the things Roxy had said about me and Mel that was untrue. Roxy told Deena that I had called her mum a *"bad mum"* and that I had called her a *"control freak"* on five separate occasions. I felt very hurt and upset by these things Roxy had said. But I was also aware of the unhealthy relationship dynamic that had developed over the years between Roxy and her mum. My intuition was that Roxy felt like she had to protect her mum. And as I'd always believed Josie had emotionally 'propped herself up' on the girls (emotional incest). Over the years this resulted in them feeling like they had to emotionally support her. I suspect our court application will have certainly tipped Josie over the edge emotionally, which will have impacted the girls. A lot of what I am talking about is psychologically very deep. We can be unaware of unhealed hurts from our past, which can affect our future relationships. A few days after I'd spoken with Deena, I took Roxy for a walk, to chat to her about some of the things she had said to Deena. It was a difficult conversation, but one I knew I needed to have. I couldn't be too hard on her because I knew she would have felt under pressure from her mum. But I knew Roxy would be defensive about what she'd said. I tried my best to be an understanding father, but I also had to make her aware that it wasn't right to lie. During our chat, it came to light that Josie had shown her text messages from me in the past and Roxy had witnessed her mum upset about them. I explained that it was wrong for her mum to show her text messages of an adult conversation. I tried to reassure Roxy by explaining to her that all she needed to know was that she had a mum who loved her very much and a dad and step-mum that loved and cared for her so much too. Roxy got upset and I could sense she felt compelled to protect her mum. It made me sad that my daughter was subconsciously carrying this unhealthy burden. It was an emotionally difficult time for both of us, but I was glad we spoke about it and it cleared the air.

Then on Monday, 13 May, the completed Section 7 report was sent to both me and Josie. This is when we discovered that Roxy had said some other things that weren't true which upset us further. Furthermore, Deena had recommended that the mid-week contact we had with the girls should stop completely. I couldn't get my head around why she would recommend this to the court? Anna had stated that she was happy with the amount of time she spends with us and Roxy had indicated that she wanted to keep one day during the week. Deena was clearly showing a bias to what mum wanted over what me and the girls were saying. The corruption was infuriating.

The narrative that was being painted by Josie and Roxy, was that mine and Roxy's relationship was contentious, which was a million miles from the truth! Deena had also spoken to Mrs James, the Child Protection Officer at Anna's School. Mrs James was clearly still aggrieved over me and Mel complaining about her assaulting Anna, six months earlier. So, she took this opportunity for retribution with both hands. Deena wrote in her report, *"Mrs Jones, the Child Protection Officer at the girls' Primary School, advised that the school have concerns about Anna's emotional presentation on certain days in school. Mrs James explained that she had spoken to Anna's class teacher in 2018 and her current class teacher, and both have recognised that Anna is unsettled and teary, lacking in concentration and will sometimes not eat her lunch on the days when Mr Kirk is collecting her from school."* I was horrified when I read what Mrs James had said. I'd had several dealings with her, so I'd experienced how she could be very rude and obnoxious, but how could she tell such lies! It was clear the picture she was trying to paint! One of the first questions I always asked the kids when I picked them from school was, *"What did you have for your dinner?"* And never once had Anna ever told me that she had not eaten her dinner. And if it was true that Anna was unsettled and teary on the days that I collected her, then why on earth had the school never informed me on those occasions? So, the next time I collected Anna from school, I decided to ask Anna's teacher if Anna was teary on the days I collected her and if there were occasions when Anna would not eat her dinner. Her teacher confirmed to me face to face, that to her knowledge, Anna was fine, and she knew nothing of what I was asking her about. This confirmed to me that Mrs James' words to Deena were a total fabrication!

Then, the day after the Section 7 report was filed, I was on my way to collect Roxy and Anna from school when I got a text message from Josie telling me that she had collected the girls early from school and that they didn't want to come for contact. She also said that they wouldn't be coming for contact that weekend and not to

Back In Court

ring her or text her back as she had now blocked me on her phone. She said she would call the police if I went to her house. I was furious and I immediately rang Deena to find out what was going on. I asked Deena how on earth Josie could be allowed to breach the court order in this way! However, Deena was unsympathetic and simply told me that I also had the right, as a father, to collect the girls from school whenever I wanted. I suspected Deena was trying to goad me into doing just that, which she knew could be perceived as though I too wasn't adhering to the court order. It confirmed to me just how sly and corrupt Deena was! She face-timed the girls later that day while they were at their mum's house. Deena later explained to me that Roxy and Anna said they didn't want to come to our house because of an incident that had happened the week before, in which I had to confiscate Roxy's mobile phone as a punishment for her behaviour. But I knew this was a convenient smokescreen for Roxy and her mum. I believed the reason Roxy didn't want to come was that she had seen the Section 7 report and would be anxious that me and Mel would want to talk to her about the things she'd said to Deena. Plus, it was only a week before the next court hearing which was convenient for Josie too. I knew she would use this to try and convince the court that my relationship with Roxy and Anna had broken down. Josie had now gained the confidence she needed to breach the court order, knowing this would be without any consequences. In fact, she now had the full support of CAFCASS to breach the order. Shocking!

The next hearing came around on the 20 May 2019 at Leeds Magistrates Court. Me and Mel represented ourselves because we didn't have a solicitor. I'd learned from eight years ago when I first took Josie to court that solicitors, in my opinion, were parasites who didn't give a rip about you or your family. It was simply about making money for them and I'd seen how they were professional liars. I wasn't too hopeful of getting what we wanted, based on Deena's recommendation. However, she had recommended that we have two consecutive weeks in the summer school holidays and an extra hour, up until 6 pm on a Sunday. Unfortunately, she had recommended that Mel's application for parental responsibility be dismissed. Once again, Deena was simply going along with what mum wanted. The hearing was short, and we agreed on an interim order before we went into the courtroom. This included that I have Roxy and Anna for just one day during the week, with the weekend contact staying the same. The magistrates set a date for a contested hearing on the 15 July 2019. This would be a half-day hearing, and both me, Mel and Deena would give evidence and the magistrates would make a new order about contact. I also learned that the magistrate's judges tended to be weak in their decision. They weren't even law experts. In fact, in a magistrate's family court, there is a bench of three judges, then a legal advisor who sits at the side to advise the magistrates on the law. It's an absolutely corrupt system! Surely the legal advisor who is an expert in the law should be the judge? I learned that any member of the public could apply to be a magistrate's judge and they only had to have a one-day law course. Madness eh!

After this hearing, I took the opportunity to sit down with Roxy and explain to her the importance of coming to spend time with us on the days she was supposed to come. I gently explained to her how important our family unit was and that it wasn't fair on any of us if she decided not to come at the last minute. She knew how we planned to do fun things as a family on the weekends that we had her and Anna. We would regularly book and pay for activities in advance and I reminded Roxy of this fact. Roxy listened and seemed to take on board what I was saying, but I got the impression that she now knew that she could do what she wanted without any consequences. I warned Roxy that there would be consequences if she were to break our agreement. Deep down I hoped she would toe the line so that I wouldn't have to follow through on my word.

Contested Hearing

Back In Court

Once again, the week before the next court hearing, Josie breached the order. On Tuesday 9 July 2019, I went to collect Roxy from school. I usually met her about one hundred metres from her school, where she would jump in my car and we would go on to collect Anna. Then we'd go get Zac, then Harlow. But on this day, there was no sign of Roxy. I waited for a while, but I had to go to collect Anna. I rang Roxy's school immediately to find out if she'd left or if she was still in school. The Head of Year confirmed that she'd definitely left school. I texted Josie, who was at work, and she replied to say she didn't know where she was either. I suspected that Roxy might have gone to her mum's house, so I drove around and knocked on the door. But there was no answer. By now, I was becoming extremely concerned, so I reported Roxy as missing. I rang the police and explained to them what had happened. Deep down, I was 90% sure that she was hiding away at her mum's. But the reality was, she was supposed to be with me, and no one knew where she was. I completed the school run and we all got home minus Roxy. About an hour later I received a phone call from the police to say they'd been to Josie's house and Roxy was there with her mum. In one sense, I was relieved that she was safe and well, but on the other hand, I was upset and disappointed that Roxy had done this. Especially after the conversation I'd had with her six weeks previously, where I'd explained to her the importance of coming on the days she was supposed to. Then on Friday afternoon that same week, I got a text message from Josie, saying that Roxy and Anna didn't want to come, so she wouldn't be sending them that weekend. Once again, Josie's timing was perfect. She'd breached the order just days before the contested hearing. She would inevitably use this to reinforce the narrative that the girls didn't want to spend time with us anymore. Furthermore, me and Mel felt we now had no option but to follow through on the consequences we'd told Roxy there would be. With all the untruths Roxy had told to Deena and now this, it felt like she was taking liberties and showing a massive lack of respect for us. And, although I knew some of her behaviour and decisions were being influenced by her mum, I also knew that Roxy was an intelligent girl who knew right from wrong. It would have been wrong of us as parents to simply let this slide, especially after everything that had gone on recently. We needed to discipline her somehow. So, we made the agonising decision not to take Roxy on holiday with us to Ibiza on the 30 July. It was a heart-wrenching decision but one we knew we had to make for Roxy's own good. No father likes or enjoys disciplining their children but just like our Father God, who often uses earthly consequences to teach and correct us, we had to do something to correct Roxy. I knew she wouldn't be happy about it and that she'd likely feel like I was being harsh, especially under the influence of her mum. Additionally, there was the issue of how we would be able to do this and still enable Anna to come away with us. I knew for a fact that if I told Josie about our decision not to take Roxy, then she would certainly prevent Anna from coming too. So, we came up with a plan that we felt could work, but it certainly wasn't failproof.

The contested hearing came around on the 15 July 2019. Me and Mel wrote up our statements beforehand, although we didn't hold much hope of keeping the midweek contact. I explained in my statement what I felt was going on concerning the psychological manipulation by Josie. I also let the court know that I'd spoken to Anna's teacher, who had confirmed to me that Anna was absolutely fine on the days I picked her up, which directly contradicted what Mrs James had told Deena. But, to my disbelief, when Deena took to the stand to give her evidence, she informed the court that she had just called Anna's school and spoken with Mrs James, who'd said she had spoken to Anna's teacher who said that she had not spoken to me at all! What on earth was going on! How could all these supposedly trusted individuals conspire in such a way, to now paint me out to be a liar! You couldn't make this up! Me and Mel were sitting in that courtroom, open-mouthed in disgust at the lies that were being spoken. I was now even more confident that the magistrates would simply go with what Deena had recommended in her Section 7 report. Sadly, that proved to be the case. However, the judge did rule that Mel could collect the girls at handovers if I informed Josie by 3 pm on a Friday we were due to have them. That was probably the only positive for us out of this whole sorry case, along with the fact that we could now take the girls on holiday abroad for two consecutive weeks. Mel also withdrew her application for parental responsibility at the hearing as it seemed highly likely that she wouldn't get it. Deena had made a recommendation in her report that Mel shouldn't be given parental responsibility. Again, just another example of Deena's strong bias towards what mum wanted. It just didn't make sense. Mel had been a loving, caring step mum to Roxy from the age of three and to Anna from birth. She'd treated them like her own and the girls adored her! Granting Mel parental responsibility should have been a no brainer. But that's just one of the problems with the family court. They are held in secret; therefore, they are not accountable for the decisions they make. In hindsight, I was naïve to think that I could get a fair decision from the family court. I'd taken confidence from the first experience in the family court in 2010, but in reality, it appeared I'd been fortunate to get a great District Judge back then who could see through Josie's games.

Chapter 16

Enough Is Enough

After the contested hearing on the 15 July, we weren't due to see Roxy and Anna until we collected them for our holiday on the 29 July. Josie made sure she took part of her holiday time with the girls so that it interfered with our contact days. She'd done this most other years as well, so it was no surprise. I was feeling apprehensive about the holiday and telling Roxy that she wasn't coming. Me and Mel came up with a plan that we felt would enable Anna to still come away with us. However, it was going to be extremely risky. The only way we felt it could work was if I told Roxy when we went to collect them, the day before our holiday to Ibiza. I'd hoped that I could get Anna in the car at the police station while telling Roxy why she wasn't coming and telling her to go and get back in her mum's car. Then we could drive home and get ready to go on holiday the next morning. It wasn't at all how I wanted to do it and I knew it would be a shock to Roxy and her mum, but I felt it just wasn't fair for Anna to miss out on a holiday simply because we were disciplining Roxy. I knew Josie wouldn't be at all happy about it and would try everything she could to stop Anna coming, which could mean she might use the police to try and stop us from going. I knew that was her style, and she certainly wouldn't just 'suck it up' and tell Roxy that she deserved to be disciplined for all the lies she'd told and for not coming for contact. In fact, it would be gold to Josie, which she could use to poison the girls against me more. I lost sleep over the decision during the two weeks leading up to our holiday and I knew we were taking a big risk. But I still felt that as a parent, discipline was important, and this was the only thing we could use as

Enough Is Enough

a punishment. It would have been so different if Roxy had lived with us full time or if me and Josie were singing from the same hymn sheet regarding parenting. Sadly, that ship had sailed a long time ago. A week before our holiday, Josie arranged with me to meet with Roxy for an hour at McDonald's. It was great to see Roxy and I took Harlow with me and they were so happy to see each other. But I knew that Josie's purpose of this meeting was for her to find out how I felt towards Roxy, given the circumstances of Josie breaching the order and the fact that Roxy didn't come for contact as she should have the previous week. I kept my mouth shut about Roxy not coming on holiday, as I knew if I gave her any inclination then Josie would certainly stop Anna coming.

The day came to collect Roxy and Anna for our holiday. I had originally arranged with Josie to collect them at 10 am on the day before our holiday, but I changed that to 5 pm. I felt it would give Josie less time to alert whoever she felt she needed to, in order to prevent Anna from coming, which would likely be Deena and the police. Our flight was at 7 am the following morning. We pulled up at the police station and as always I waited for Josie to arrive with the girls. I was super nervous about how this was going to play out. Josie arrived and the girls came over to my car. It was a warm, summer evening and Mel was in the passenger seat with Zac and Harlow in the back. We'd told Zac some weeks before that Roxy wasn't coming so he knew the drill. I gave them both a big hug and Anna got in the car. I put my arm around Roxy and explained that she wasn't coming away and briefly explained the reasons why. But then Josie set off in her car, more quickly than I'd anticipated. I had to flag her down to stop and told Roxy to get in her mum's car. As soon as Josie realised what was going on, she erupted with rage. She screamed, *"If Roxy's not going, Anna's not going either!!"*

I'd already jumped back in my car and was driving away when Josie put her hands on my bonnet as I was driving away in a desperate attempt to stop me. There was a set of traffic lights at the entrance of the police station car park which was on red. As I sat waiting for them to change, I could see in my rearview mirror that Josie was in full drama mode behaving like a frantic lunatic, on the phone, jumping up and down as she tried to get the attention of two police cars that had just entered the station. She was shouting at them, *"Stop that car! He's taking my baby!"* That's all I needed, I thought to myself, as I willed the lights to change to green. Before I knew it two police cars were surrounding me. I knew the plan had failed and Anna had no chance of coming on holiday with us now. I calmly stepped out of my car and explained the situation to the officers. I showed them the text message conversation from months earlier, showing me and Josie arranging the holiday and a copy of the court order. I'd been here before though, so I knew that the police always favoured the mum in these situations, so I held little hope that they would let us leave with Anna. It's a bias that still needs addressing and sadly it exists in all areas of our society. As I've said before, it's my opinion, that a mum's rights always trump the father's rights, which is so wrong. At this stage, Anna was visibly upset, and Mel was trying to console her and reassure her that everything was going to be OK. Anna had just witnessed her mum attempt to stop a moving car and act like a crazed lunatic! The police took Josie and Roxy into the station and asked us to drive back into the car park while they did their enquiries. Mel was hopeful we would be able to take Anna, but I knew it was just a matter of time. After about an hour, a police officer asked if they could speak to Anna. She had calmed down by now, but I knew she would say she wanted to go with her mum. Thirty minutes later, a police officer came out and told us we were free to go and that Anna was going with her mum. When I questioned how they had come to their decision, the officer told me that he should really arrest me as Josie had alleged that I had assaulted her. I wasn't in the least bit surprised. That was exactly her style. The police officer suspected she was lying, otherwise, they would have certainly arrested me. To this day, I don't fully know what Josie alleged I did to her, but I reckon she told the police that I tried to run her over. So, we drove home, and I was so upset that

Anna wasn't coming and how the whole situation had unfolded. This drama could likely emotionally scar the girls. The holiday to Ibiza just wasn't the same without Roxy and Anna, but we made the most of it and we had a great holiday. However, it was during the holiday that I started to grieve for the girls. I'd never experienced grief like this before and I knew deep down that I might not see Roxy and Anna for some time. My sleep was badly affected, and I was hurting emotionally, not just for me but for them and us as a family. As the following weeks and months passed by, I began to experience this grief on a deeper level. At times it felt like an emotional rollercoaster.

On our return from our holiday, we weren't due to have the girls until the weekend of the 3 September. However, I wasn't hopeful that Josie would turn up with them. In fact, I expected that I would have to apply back to the court if I were ever to see Roxy and Anna again. My concerns became reality and Josie breached the order by not making the girls available on both weekends we were supposed to have them in September. I turned up at the police station at 6 pm on Friday and waited on both occasions, but Josie didn't show up. I decided that my only chance to ever see Roxy and Anna again was to make an application to enforce the order. I also arranged a meeting with Mr Bamgill, the headteacher at Anna's school. The purpose of the meeting was to explain to him that because I would no longer be collecting Anna from school, I wanted to reiterate to him the importance of them sending me correspondence about school performances, sports days, etc. It was also a few days after Anna's birthday, so I took her birthday card with me in the hope that I could hand it to her. When I got to the school, Mr Bamgill informed me that Mrs James and Anna's teacher would be in the meeting too. I told him in no uncertain terms that Mrs James could not be in this meeting. I told him that she had done enough damage to my family. The very sight of that woman would have caused my blood to boil! Mr Bamgill came back and said he'd asked Mrs James to leave. So, I sat down and explained the situation, then I asked him if I could hand Anna her birthday card. He said he would have to go and ask Mrs James if this was OK. So off he went. I knew there was no chance that bitter, sour woman would let me hand my own daughter her birthday card. When he came back, he told me that I could not give Anna her card but that he could hand the card to Anna for me. I was furious, but I managed to remain calm. I explained to him that the school was breaking the law according to The Children's Act 1989, in preventing me, as a father with parental responsibility, from handing Anna a card. He said the reason was that it was not my day for contact, according to the most recent court order. To which, I asked him that if this was the case, then why had the school allowed Josie to collect Anna a few months earlier on a day when it was not Josie's day for contact? I asked him how he couldn't comprehend that this was a blatant case of double standards and that they were being prejudiced against me as a father. But he sat there and said nothing. I believe he knew it was wrong. Inside, I was raging! I wanted to smash him and Mrs James' face to pieces. But instead, I sat there, stared into his eyes, and let him feel the awkward silence. My last words to him before I gave him Anna's birthday card and walked out were, *"You don't give a s**t, do you?"*

The injustice of everything I'd gone through over the past year was overwhelming. I took to the social media site, Twitter, to vent my frustrations about the way the school was treating me as a father. Plus, I knew Mr Bamgill hated any bad publicity on Twitter. Some years before, me and Mel had posted on Twitter about how the school was deliberately not telling me about Anna's school performance's after they failed to tell me about her Christmas Nativity, which I ended up missing. At the time, he begged us to take the posts down, but we refused. My recent posts worked a treat, and about three days after I exposed the school on Twitter for breaking the law, I received a phone call from the police. They explained to me that Mr Bamgill had reported me for harassment and complained about my Twitter posts. The police warned me about my posts, but I felt I had not said anything that was breaking the law. It just confirmed to me how pathetic Mr Bamgill and Mrs James were behaving. I must have been a real pain in the backside to them and they were out to silence me! But I wasn't intimidated by their feeble attempts to shut me up. Their actions were so wrong and unprofessional on every level. Injustice is something that I just can't stomach. It rocks me to my core, whether it's against myself or someone else. However, sometime later, I realised that as a follower of Jesus, I had disobeyed God's Word. In my anger and frustration about the way I was being treated as a father, I had veered off track. Jesus tells us in Matthew 5:43-44 *"You have heard that it was said, 'Love your neighbour and hate your enemy. But I tell you, love your enemies and pray for those who persecute you'"*.

But at that moment, I just could not find it in me to love my enemies and pray for them. I was acting out of my fleshly desire to expose them for the wrong they were doing to me. Being a follower of Jesus can be so difficult at times, but I also know my God is a God of grace and he sympathises with the struggles we go through. Jesus should have been my example in that situation, after all, He was tortured and brutally killed on the Cross, but in that moment, he still found it in him to forgive those that killed him.

Hearing

We got a relatively swift court date at Leeds Magistrates court on the 15 October 2019. However, we only received three days' notice of the hearing. To be honest, I wasn't too hopeful about my application, having been through the court process already over the past nine months. I decided to get in touch with a McKenzie Friend. Their role is to assist people in court cases, but they are not solicitors or barristers. They do usually charge a fixed fee, but it is a fraction of the fee that a solicitor would charge. I felt I needed someone who had experience in the family court and that had some knowledge of the law. So, I got in touch with a lady who was experienced in the family court and had experience with parental alienation cases. She put me in touch with a McKenzie Friend based in Leicester called

Amanda. She agreed to come and assist me at the hearing for which I was extremely grateful for, as it was only at a day's notice. She seemed to know her stuff and was fully aware of how prevalent parental alienation was.

During this hearing, Josie and her solicitor gave their excuses for breaching the order on the fact that the girls no longer wanted to see us because they were still so upset about the holiday incident. They created the narrative of me being a bad guy and they blamed everything that happened on me, and consequently, the girls no longer want to see us anymore. It's what I expected them to say. The court accepted Josie's reason for breaching the order and instructed CAFCASS to do an Addendum report to ascertain Roxy and Anna's 'wishes and feelings' on the matter. This report was to be completed within eight weeks. The next court date was set for the 20 December and in the meantime, I was only allowed to have indirect contact with the girls in the form of writing them letters every two weeks. What a joke! Nine years of having 50/50 shared care and now the court was saying I couldn't see them at all. Just another example of the imbalance of justice that exists in the family courts towards fathers. This was the worst thing that could have happened. It would give Josie uninterrupted time with the girls and enable her to project her negative views of me onto them. I had already sent the girls two letters by this point and I'd had no reply. I knew things were looking grim as I was 99% sure that the girls were going to tell Deena that they didn't want to see me anymore. Even if they did want to see me, they were always going to say what they felt Josie wanted them to say, as they were now so heavily aligned with their mum. As a father, my heart was breaking for them, but also Zac and Harlow. Harlow had gone from having her sisters there half the time to not seeing them at all. She was only five years old and didn't fully understand why her sisters had suddenly gone. There were times when I would put her to bed, and we would pray for Roxy and Anna. Harlow would get upset and ask me why her sisters didn't come anymore. All I could say to help her understand was that their mum was being mean. It wasn't fair on any of the kids and throughout all this, the family courts and CAFCASS simply referred to Zac and Harlow as 'Non-Subject Children'. What on earth does that mean? They basically didn't exist to the court. So sad!

After this latest hearing, I got in touch with a more local McKenzie Friend named David. He was recommended through a father's group I was a part of, which was a branch off of Fathers4Justice. You may know them as the guys that made a name for themselves by climbing up and onto buildings dressed as superheroes. It was through this group that I discovered there were hundreds of other fathers who were in a similar position to me. So many good fathers that were being separated from their children because of bitter, twisted, ex-partners and a broken court system that was supporting these mothers. Some of their stories made my situation look tame. David told me that he'd dealt with cases where there was extreme hostility between parents, but he had always been able to help the parent he was representing to maintain contact with their children. He advised me to write a letter of apology to Josie for taking her to court. His purpose for this was to try and soften her up. He thought the only chance I had of seeing the girls again was to butter up Josie. But unfortunately, he didn't know Josie as I did. He didn't realise that her ultimate goal had always been to eliminate me from the girl's lives forever. And Josie knew full well that all the cards were now stacked in her favour and that she could do as she pleased. She had seen first-hand how biased CAFCASS and the courts were towards her and she was on a roll! However, I took on board David's advice and he helped me write an apology letter to Josie. It was difficult as I didn't want to sell my soul by being phoney and it did feel very derived. I mean how do you apologise to someone who is stopping you being a father to your children? It just didn't sit right with me. But his theory was that it was also for CAFCASS and the court to see as well. A few weeks after this hearing, me and Mel were invited to go and speak to Deena at the CAFCASS offices in Leeds. I wasn't particularly looking forward to this meeting. It was all very fake. I did my best to be nice and polite to Deena, but really, I just wanted to tell her exactly what I thought of her. I felt she was a big reason why I was no longer seeing Roxy and Anna. I honestly don't know how people like her sleep at night, knowing that they are effectively eliminating a good father from a child's life. How can anyone believe that it is healthy for a child? But I knew I had to play it cool, nod and smile and hope that somewhere inside Deena there was a heart. I told her that it was a mistake not to take Roxy on holiday. To be honest, though, I said it off the back of David's advice. In hindsight, I should have approached the holiday situation differently. Maybe it was harsh to have Roxy miss out on a holiday. But what happened, happened, and whoever was to blame, I just wanted to find a way to move forward with the girls.

A few weeks after our meeting, she completed her Addendum report. The report was conclusive, in the fact that both Roxy and Anna were saying that they didn't want to see us again. It didn't come as a shock. Deena's recommendation to the court was that I only am allowed indirect contact in the form of a letter once a month. It also came to light in her report that Anna was not even reading anything I had sent to her. That was genuinely concerning to me and I felt there was something psychological going on there. For Anna, a 9-year-old girl who had only ever had a close, loving relationship with me, Mel, Zac and Harlow, to be refusing to even read anything I was sending, was strange, to say the least. Furthermore, it showed me that Josie certainly wasn't encouraging her to read the letters and for them to reply. If it had been the other way around, I would be telling the girls that they had to write back to their mum. It would be non-negotiable. It's basic manners in my book!

A few days before the next hearing, I went along to Anna's school Christmas performance. I was excited to go and see her for the first time in nearly five months. I got there about ten minutes early and took my seat in the hall with some of the other parents. As soon as Josie saw me, she rushed off out of the hall and didn't come back in until just before the show was about to start. I thought it was strange behaviour. Anyway, Anna came out with her classmates and sang her heart out. It was great to see her and she looked even more grown-up than the last time I had seen her. I even got a video of her towards the end of her performance. She looked over at me and smiled and waved at her mum. She looked content and I was glad she had seen me there. Then later that evening I saw two emails from Josie's solicitor. One had been sent the night before. The email was her solicitor telling me not to go to the school to watch Anna's performance. She said that the school, Deena and Josie had all discussed the matter and felt that it was best for Anna if I didn't go, as it could upset Anna. This was the first I'd heard of this and I'd had no contact from Deena or the school about it. Wow! Josie wasn't satisfied with me not having any direct contact with the girls, she also wanted to control and stop me from simply going to watch Anna's school performance. Now, I knew Josie had some issues, but this was another level of control she was seeking. I was just so glad that I hadn't seen the email before I went to watch Anna. I would still have gone, but I would have been apprehensive about it. Then the second email that was sent after Anna's morning performance was just as shocking. Her solicitor wrote at the beginning of the email,

"Dear Mr Kirk, we have been advised by the school that despite our email and the school's own discussions with you, you attended Anna's Christmas performance. This has caused a significant amount of upset and distress to Anna prior to her performance."

I was flabbergasted! The lies were unreal. There were no discussions between me and school! In fact, I had emailed Mr Bamgill a few weeks early, asking him to send me the dates of Anna's Christmas performances. And he sent them to me. That's how I knew the dates and times of her school performances. It just proved to me once again how solicitors can be professional liars! I really wanted to reply to the solicitor and Mel even drafted a reply email. But I spoke with David, who advised me not to reply. He told me that solicitors don't decide who can go to a school performance and he said that solicitors tend to do this sort of thing to distress people, especially close to a hearing. So, I took his advice and I didn't reply.

The next court hearing on the 20 December was a farce. It ended up being a non-hearing. The magistrates wouldn't allow my McKenzie Friend to address the court. Between them and the court legal advisor, they didn't seem to know what the law was regarding a McKenzie Friend. So, I appealed the decision not to let David address the court which meant it would get escalated to a District Judge at a future hearing. I didn't mind this at all. Over the past twelve months, I'd found the Magistrates judges to have no backbone whatsoever and they simply bowed down to CAFCASS and the mum. It was also at this hearing that I found out that Josie wanted to make me pay for her legal fees and wanted to prevent me making any more court applications for the next twelve months. Wow! She'd obviously gained so much confidence that the courts were on her side that she dared to ask for the court to make me pay her legal fees. Either that, or she was running out of money to pay her solicitor. Personally, I couldn't comprehend paying my hard-earned money on trying to separate my kids from a good parent. That's some deep acrimony there! She also objected to me obtaining the CCTV from the police station car park from the day before we went on holiday. Her solicitor claimed that by me requesting the CCTV, it would further damage my relationship with the girls. But by now I'd got used to solicitors' bulls**t talk! Simply put, Josie didn't want the CCTV to be made available because she knew it would show her acting like a crazed lunatic in the presence of the kids. It would also show that she was lying about me assaulting her. It was at this hearing that I received a heart-warming text message from Zac. Zac has always been a great kid and we are awfully close. He was very switched on emotionally for his age. He sent me such a sweet message that got me choked up, but it really lifted my spirits. He wrote, *"Love you dad, u r amazing and I hope court goes well. You deserve to be loved. xxx"*

Chapter 17

Final Nail In The Coffin

The next court hearing was scheduled for the 14 January 2020. This time it would be in front of a district judge at Leeds County Court. It gave me a little bit more hope, as I'd previously had more success with a district judge. But I wasn't holding my breath. By now, I had written seven letters to Roxy and Anna since September and still had no reply. I knew Roxy was receiving my letters because I always sent them to Roxy's school Head of Year, who always confirmed he'd handed them to her. At the October hearing, Josie wanted me to send any letters directly to her, but I insisted that I send them through Roxy's school. I knew Josie would inspect any letters that I sent before giving them to Roxy and Anna or even prevent them from receiving my letters. It was this Head of Year who told me Roxy had broken her wrist whilst at a trampoline park outside of school time. To me, that just showed even more so, the lack of respect that Josie had for me, as Roxy's dad, she didn't have the decency to inform me that my daughter had broken her wrist. She also didn't tell me when she moved Roxy to a different high school at the start of year eight.

I wasn't happy with the advice my McKenzie Friend was giving me. He basically wanted me to say that everything was my fault and that I caused it all, by making the application to enforce the order. I was growing weary of his weak strategy to gain back contact with the girls, which was clearly not working. I began to see his lack of integrity. He thought that the court wouldn't take any notice of my claims that Josie had manipulated the girls over the years. I understood his point, but for me, I had to be honest and stand by my own convictions. It didn't sit right with me to tell lies about myself and pretend I was in the wrong when I wasn't. He drafted me a position statement for the upcoming hearing which he sent me by email to check over. What he wrote left me seething! He was massively misrepresenting me, and I told him I wasn't happy. I altered the position statement, and he came along with me to the hearing. But in the back of my mind, I knew I wouldn't be using his services for the next hearing. I expected that this would be a preliminary hearing for a contested hearing in about six to eight weeks. The judge allowed David to address the court on my behalf. It turned out to be a Deputy District judge. But she was no better than any of the magistrate's judges. She picked up on something Roxy had said to Deena in the Addendum report, which read

> *"I've read all of Dad's letters. He's trying to reel us in with these letters but it's not going to take a few words to get us back. I probably will never trust him again. It doesn't sound like my Dad and I think someone's helping him to write the letters, it doesn't sound like him. I ask Anna if she wants to read them, but she always says no."*

I knew Roxy's words were likely influenced by what she'd heard her mum say. However, the judge started giving me a lecture, telling me the letters needed to be my own words and written by me. I sat in disbelief as I listened to her, but after a while, I had to stop her. I interrupted her to put her straight. I sternly told her that all the letters were in fact, my own words, and written by me. Judges hate it when you dare to answer them back. I'd learned over the past twelve months that they like to feel important and flaunt their position of authority over you. The whole courtroom atmosphere is very fake. It always felt like a show, where everyone was acting, rather than being their authentic selves. Then, Josie's solicitor suggested that it might make a difference if I were to write a letter to Roxy, with the help of Deena, apologising to her for not taking her on holiday.

Ironically, the judge agreed. After she'd just berated me for not writing the letters myself, she now wanted Deena to help me write one. Unbelievable, they couldn't even see their own contradiction! Plus, the first letter I wrote to Roxy and Anna back in September, I had sympathised with Roxy about my decision not to take her on holiday. I wrote,

> *"I miss you and love you so, sooo, much! It hurts that I hear you don't want to see me at the moment. But I respect your wishes…… I also want you to know what a difficult decision it was for me not to take you on holiday. I love our family holidays. I don't blame you if you're upset about that".*

So, I agreed to write another letter, apologising to Roxy. However, I knew it wouldn't make a blind bit of difference. It was Josie and Deena's way of making me jump through another hoop, to give them time to find another hoop for me to jump through. A date was set for a contested hearing which would be on the 27 February 2020. That would be the seventh hearing in twelve months.

I searched the internet to find another McKenzie Friend to help me in the contested hearing. I found a lady named Claire, who was based in Manchester. I spoke to her on the phone and we arranged to meet up. She seemed to immediately get a good grasp of our case. She had over five years' experience in the family court as a McKenzie Friend. She also had a law degree and was studying to be a solicitor. I also liked the fact that she agreed with my decision not to take Roxy on holiday as a way of disciplining her. She could see straight away, from reading the initial Section 7 report and the addendum report, how the girls were being influenced by Josie's attitude. She pointed out to me that the girls had gone from wanting and enjoying their time with us, to literally hating us within the space of six months. After my previous McKenzie Friend, I was so glad that Claire and I were on the same page. She helped me to prepare a position statement for the contested hearing and the questions for cross-examining Deena and Josie. As was agreed in court, I sent Roxy and Anna a sincere letter and this time I actually received a reply letter from Roxy. However, I knew this was because the court had ordered Deena to speak to the girls about my letter and was going to encourage them to reply. But Josie got in first and she enticed Roxy to reply to me before the date Deena was due to speak to the girls. The letter from Roxy was very negative and she basically reiterated what she had said to Deena in the Addendum report. She repeated her feelings about never wanting to see me again, telling me that I still hadn't apologised.

The morning of the contested hearing came around and I was incredibly nervous. I knew this could be the last chance for my relationship with Roxy and Anna. From my previous twelve months experience, my faith in the family law system was at zero. My only real hope of seeing the girls again was if I got a wise judge who could see the truth of what was going on. It was a full day hearing and the format would be that Deena would give her evidence first, then I would have the chance to cross-examine her. Then I would be in the stand, where Josie's solicitor would cross-examine me. Finally, I would get the chance to cross-examine Josie.

It was a different judge again. I asked him if Claire would be allowed to speak and do the cross-examining, but the judge dismissed my request. He said that only in exceptional circumstances would a McKenzie Friend be allowed to address the court. So, it was all down to me to do the cross-examining, which was a daunting task. Deena gave her evidence first. There wasn't much she said that I wasn't expecting. She basically repeated what she wrote in her Addendum report. I questioned her about why she had not taken my concerns about Josie manipulating the girls seriously and why she had not followed the parental alienation framework that CAFCASS have available. I questioned her about why she had spoken to the girls on many occasions whilst at their mum's house, as she must have known that the girl's responses would be influenced by mum's presence. I pointed out that the only time that both Roxy and Anna said they wanted to keep contact, was when she spoke to them at school, away from Josie. Deena stuttered her way through that question. Overall, I was happy with how the cross-examination went. Then, it was my turn to speak. I was conscious of making sure I was my authentic self and that I spoke from the heart with confidence and conviction. I felt I did just that. My thinking was that if I ended up not seeing the girls again, I wanted to be able to walk away, knowing that I had told the judge everything I knew and believed to be true about this whole situation. Whether he believed me or not was out of my hands. I knew the trick was not to fall into the solicitor's trap of just answering their questions with short answers. It was important I elaborated and told the court what I wanted them to know about the situation. I'd learned this from the employment tribunal against Salford, some years before, when their barrister had a field day on me.

So, after I was cross-examined, we retired for lunch. But I was happy with how I presented myself and the things I said. Then it was Josie's turn to be cross-examined. I could tell she was nervous. The judge even had to tell her to slow down when she was confirming her name and address. Again, the questions that Claire had prepared were excellent. Unfortunately, the judge stopped me asking a couple of questions, one of which was, *"If the girls said they wanted to live with me, would you let them?"* and *"If the girls said they didn't want to go to school anymore, would you let them?"*

You see, Josie was hiding behind the girls stated wishes and feelings, so her angle was always going to be, *"I just want whatever the girls want"*. Very clever, given the fact that the girls were now aligned with her. I was disappointed that the judge stopped me from asking these questions, as we had a whole line of questioning which followed on from these questions. At about ten to four in the afternoon, we retired for a break while the judge made his decision. However, I got the sense that things were not going my way. We went back in to hear District Judge Trey sum up and give his decision. He waffled on for about thirty minutes before he got to his decision. After he'd been speaking for about five minutes, I knew his decision was going to go against me. He proceeded to verbally rebuke me about several things. To my disbelief, he heavily criticised me for going to Anna's school Christmas performance. What the heck!! I couldn't believe it! What planet was this guy on! He said that I should have known Anna would be upset to see her dad there. But the fact was she wasn't upset, and I even had video evidence of her smiling and waving as she came off the stage. It was just another example of how a mother's word is taken as gospel in the family court. He also heavily criticised me for the content of my apology letter to the girls. My letter read,

Dear Roxy and Anna,

I wanted to write you both this letter to tell you how very sorry I am about how things have turned out.

Roxy, my intention was never to hurt or upset you, but I don't blame you for being upset with me. It was an extremely difficult decision for me not to take you on holiday. I take responsibility for the part I played in that. We all know how much we love and enjoy our family holidays.

The decision not to take you on holiday was because as your dad, it is part of my job to teach you right from wrong. As parents, it is our job to teach our children not to lie. If you do something wrong in life, there are consequences. Consequences might include having something taken away, like a phone, an earlier bedtime or a day trip away. In your case, it was the holiday. This is all a part of learning. You are getting older now Roxy and it's important you take on all these little teaching moments and allow them to build you into a better person.

Anna, I am very sorry for the upset that the whole situation has caused you. I did not ever want you to be caught up in all of this. I

truly want you to know that you did nothing wrong. Every choice I make is because I know you are both amazing girls and I want you both to be the best you can possibly be. You are two very different girls and both of you are beautiful in your own way!

Anna, I wanted you to still come on holiday, as something your sister did should not affect you. I also apologise to you for everything that happened that day. I think both myself and your mum could have handled the situation better.

It's been almost six months now since that happened. I'd hoped that with time you would be able to understand why I made the decision I did.

I miss you and love you both so very much! I do respect both your wishes.

Do you like all the pictures Harlow has drawn for you? She loves doing them. She misses her big sister's so much. She asks about you both a lot!

I will always be your dad and I will always love you both with every bit of my heart.

Did you like all the family photos I have been sending you of the great times we've all had over the years and the pictures of the things we have all been doing recently?

Love you always, Dad. x x x x

I knew Josie, Deena and the judge would have preferred me to write a grovelling letter to the girls, telling Roxy she'd done nothing wrong, and that it was all my fault that they were now so upset. But I've never been one to conform and that would have been so wrong of me. What message would that have sent to Roxy? As a parent, I had to do what I thought was the right thing and stick to my beliefs and convictions. And through all this, Josie had never once acknowledged that she had done anything wrong. The judge's words and the decision just confirmed to me that as a father, if you dare to upset your children by disciplining them, then CAFCASS and the court instantly label you as a bad parent. Crazy, eh? The judge ordered what he called a twelve-month monitor order. He had basically followed what Deena had recommended and I was only allowed to have indirect contact by writing a letter to the girls once a month. The monitor order meant that if Josie did not encourage the girls to make direct contact with me, then I could go back to court in twelve months and make another application. But this was a total cop-out by the judge in my opinion. I could accept that Roxy was now thirteen and was free to make her own decisions about contact, but Anna was only nine. I sat and shook my head as the judge read out his decision, which he took offence to. He made a disapproving comment to me, but inside my blood was boiling and I couldn't stop myself piping up, *"Well done, I hope you're satisfied with yourself! You have just left two girls without a father!"* Claire was sitting next to me and punched me in the arm, trying to get me to shut up. But right there and then, I didn't care if I got banged up for contempt of court. What that judge had just ordered was criminal in my book and I had to let him know.

I walked out of the courthouse, feeling utterly dejected and it felt as if I'd just gone twelve rounds with Anthony Joshua. Zac phoned me to see how things had gone. While I was telling him about the judge's decision, all my emotion welled up inside me and I began to sob uncontrollably. When I heard Zac's voice, it all hit me. I felt like I'd let him and Harlow down. They loved their sisters so much and they were all so close. It wasn't just me that was affected, they would likely never see their sisters again now. The reality set in that I may never see Roxy and Anna again. But I knew I had to somehow find the positives out of all of this. Mel, Zac and Harlow had been my source of strength throughout all this. I had the option of appealing the court's decision, but what was the point! I was fighting a system that was so against fathers. It would be a complete waste of time, energy, and money. I'd spent the last year fighting a broken, corrupt system. I'd just about had all the fight beaten out of me. The system had brought me to my knees emotionally. Even if I did make a successful appeal, Josie knew the court orders meant nothing and that she could breach them at will. They simply weren't worth the paper they were written on.

Chapter 18

Hopes For The Future

The prospect of reuniting with Roxy and Anna and rebuilding our relationship look slim at this moment. Just getting a letter or a birthday card to them is a challenge now. It sometimes feels like the devil has a ring around them, stopping me from having any contact. Over the weeks following the last court hearing, I confided in some trusted friends and I decided the right thing to do was to keep reaching out to them by writing letters. I hope that one day, their eyes will be opened to the truth. I love them dearly, I always will and all I have ever wanted is what is best for them. As a father I am not perfect, I have made mistakes, but my heart simply wants what is best for them. My desire has always been to give all my children the best possible start in life, teach them right from wrong, protect and lead and guide them to their best life. Just like our Father God desires for us. But I'm also aware that some of the things they have been exposed to over the years could cause them psychological and mental issues as they grow into their adulthood. Although Roxy and Anna are now without their earthly father, they still have a heavenly Father who loves them so much more than I ever could. I will always pray for them. God gives us many promises in his word. One particular Bible verse that people don't display as bumper stickers is this one, in John 16:33, where Jesus says,

"I've told you all this so that trusting me, you will be unshakable and assured, deeply at peace. In this Godless world, you will continue to

experience trials and sorrows. But take heart! I have conquered the world".

I've certainly experienced my fair share of trials and sorrows. However, I am also grateful for the many ways God has blessed me. I have an amazing wife in Mel and four amazing kids. Albeit two have been taken away for now, but I must focus on the family I do have and who love me dearly. I also have to lean on God's promise in Romans 8:28, where the apostle Paul wrote,

"And we know that God causes everything to work together for the good of those who love God and are called according to his purpose for them"

At this moment in time, I cannot see how God is working all this together for my good, but I still believe He will. I recall all the times in my life when God has come through and blessed me, even when I was at my wit's end. He has always been there to strengthen, encourage and comfort me. I've also come to realise that what is happening is very much a spiritual battle. Jesus says in John 10:10,

"The thief's purpose is to kill, steal and destroy. But my purpose is to give them a rich and satisfying life"

The devil hates families and wants to separate them for good. But I know that God is good, and He has an eternal plan for me and my family. I find hope in standing on God's promises, one of which is in Deuteronomy 30:2-4,

"God, your God, will restore everything you lost; He'll have compassion on you; He'll come back and pick up the pieces from all the places where you were scattered. No matter how far away you end up, God, your God, will get you out of there"

I have also been putting a lot of my energy into the father's group I am a part of. The goal has always been to petition for a change in the family law system in order to get a starting point of 50/50 shared care when parents separate. This model has proven to be effective in many Scandinavian countries and has proved that children do better in all aspects of life when they have a meaningful relationship with both parents. The statistics are undeniable about how children who have a loving, meaningful relationship with both parents are so much happier and stable in every area of their lives as they grow into adulthood.

Me, Mel, Zac and Harlow went to Downing Street in August 2020 to take part in a protest. There are so many hurting fathers and children who fall victim to the biased family courts. So many good fathers are being separated from their children for no apparent reason. It is a horrendous system as I know all too well. However, fighting for change in the world's system can be draining, so I have to have the wisdom to know when to take a step back. But anything I can do to make a difference and to help other fathers who have been through or are going through what I've experienced, I genuinely want to help.

Although my heart breaks that I am not a part of Roxy and Anna's life at the moment, I feel blessed. Blessed with the family I do have. I'm so grateful to God for all the amazing memories that we made over the years. We packed so much fun and laughter into the family times we had. I recently made a video that is available on YouTube, titled 'A Kirk Family Tribute' which perfectly sums up how I feel about my family and the amazing times we've had. I hope Roxy and Anna will see this video one day and remember all the great memories we made.

Hopes For The Future

Me, Mel, Zac and Harlow went to protest on Downing Street in August 2020

About The Author

Andy Kirk is a former Leeds Rhinos Rugby League player, the founder of Porn on the Brain; a ministry outreach which aims to educate the youth of today and others of the dangers of pornography, both psychological and emotional, and the owner of Born Again Sports Therapy.

He retired from professional rugby in 2009 after a successful career spanning over 12 years.

Andy is actively trying to bring awareness of the British family court systems to the government and believes strongly, alongside others who work within the family court legal system, that the Scandinavian family court system is more beneficial to children of separated parents, emotionally, psychologically and relationally. He is currently working with groups focusing on father's rights in hope to ensure a legal change is made in this court system.

Andy lives with his wife Mel and two of his children in the north of England.

You can contact him on andykirk82@hotmail.co.uk

Printed in Poland
by Amazon Fulfillment
Poland Sp. z o.o., Wrocław